T0013328

TEMPLE
LAMP

ADVANCE PRAISE FOR THE BOOK

'Maaz Bin Bilal's *Temple Lamp* is the long-awaited translation, into English, of one of the most extraordinary and important poems written in India during the 19th century—*Chiragh-e-Dair*. Composed in exquisite Farsi, it is the great Urdu poet Ghalib's paean of praise and declaration of love for the city of Banaras. Arriving there in the spring of 1827, the 30-year-old Ghalib fell in love with this ancient and ever-renewed city, at once a setting for the spiritual quest and a pageant of worldly delights. Wandering through its gardens and bazaars, pausing at its temples and savouring the festivities of its ghats, Ghalib stayed in Banaras for three months. He chose, very deliberately, to write his *masnavi* for the city in 108 verses, a number auspicious to Shaiva and Vaishnava alike. Maaz Bin Bilal brings across the mystical exaltation and sensuous excitement that Ghalib experienced in Banaras. In this gifted translator's handling, we find our consciousness magically refreshed. We marvel at the capacious imagination of a 19th-century poet who embraced the plurality of his country's traditions, the cross-pollinating diversity of its belief systems and idioms of everyday life. In retrieving *Chiragh-e-Dair* at this present moment of darkness and turbulence, Maaz Bin Bilal summons us into the presence of a 'Temple Lamp' that casts its illumination upon all of us, regardless of what inherited identity or location we may represent. This splendid translation shows us the way back to a past of shared relationships and lovingly nurtured dialogue, and also to a future when we may be healed of the divisions that we have inflicted upon ourselves.'

—Ranjit Hoskote, Poet and Translator

'*Chiragh-e-Dair*, a Persian *masnavi* by Ghalib, is perhaps the greatest poem ever written on the holy city of Benaras in any language. Through a series of subtle and complex images, exquisite nuances, unmistakable resonances, Ghalib celebrates, adores, explores and articulates the beauty, the ancientness, the spiritual ethos, the sensuous presence and grandeur of a great city. And its life line the river Ganga.

Temple Lamp is both a communicative and faithful translation in English. The Lamp, coincidentally, also throws light on how a great modernist poet in Urdu and Persian was able to capture the abiding sacred enchantment and the rich natural wealth of a holy city of Hinduism while being a Muslim.'

—Ashok Vajpeyi,
Poet and Literary-Cultural Critic

'In his lively, readable, well-annotated interpretation of *Chiragh-e-Dair*, Maaz Bin Bilal shows us how keenly the young Ghalib enjoyed his stay in Banaras—and how much he felt it as an almost illicit escape from his life in Delhi. For the newcomer, he also provides an extensive and helpful introduction. His work is the best available overview of this unusual Persian *masnavi*.'

—Frances Pritchett
Professor Emerita of Modern Indic Languages
Columbia University

'Translating [the works of] Ghalib whether from Persian or Urdu into English has never been easy. Nonetheless, brave translators who take on this challenge must be applauded. Maaz Bin Bilal's rendition of Ghalib's celebrated narrative poem *Chiragh-e-Dair* is a step towards opening a treasure [trove] of beautiful *masnavis* that are some of the finest in the Persian classical tradition. Bilal prefaces his translation with a comprehensive introduction that provides much needed context to the poem, and to Ghalib's poetics.'

—Mehr Afshan Farooqi,
Professor, Department of Middle Eastern and
South Asian Languages and Cultures,
University of Virginia

'Here at last is a lucid and superbly researched English translation of Ghalib's famous *masnavi* on Banaras. The translation lets us experience how Ghalib envisioned the beauties and pleasures of Banaras in line with an old Persian-Arabic geographical tradition of celebrating the virtues of a city and its people, inscribing Banaras into a Persianate literary tradition of validating civic flourishing as paradise on earth.'

—Prashant Keshavmurthy,
Associate Professor of Persian-Iranian Studies
Institute of Islamic Studies, McGill University

Dr Maaz Bin Bilal ne ek bada kaam kiya hai. Is aandhi mein Chiragh-e-Dair ko bujhne se bacha liya. Banaras ko 'mandir ka diya' kehne wale Mirza Ghalib the. Farsi mein likhi is nazm ko angrezi mein tarjumah karke Dr Maaz ne baaqi duniya ke saare saahil khol diye hain.

—Gulzar,
Poet, Lyricist, and Film-maker

[Dr Maaz Bin Bilal has completed a work of immense importance. During this storm, he has saved the 'Temple Lamp' from blowing out. It was Ghalib who called Banaras 'a temple lamp'. By translating this Persian poem into English, Dr Maaz has unlocked the shores of the rest of the world.]

MIRZA GHALIB

TEMPLE
LAMP
Verses on Banaras

Translated from the Persian and
with an Introduction by
Maaz Bin Bilal

PENGUIN BOOKS
An imprint of Penguin Random House

PENGUIN BOOKS

USA | Canada | UK | Ireland | Australia
New Zealand | India | South Africa | China

Penguin Books is part of the Penguin Random House group of companies
whose addresses can be found at global.penguinrandomhouse.com

Published by Penguin Random House India Pvt. Ltd
4th Floor, Capital Tower 1, MG Road,
Gurugram 122 002, Haryana, India

First published in English in Penguin Books by Penguin Random House India 2022

Introduction and English translation copyright © Maaz Bin Bilal 2022

All rights reserved

10 9 8 7 6 5 4 3 2

This is a work of fiction. Names, characters, places and incidents are either the
product of the author's imagination or are used fictitiously, and any resemblance
to any actual person, living or dead, events or locales is entirely coincidental.

ISBN 9780670094325

Typeset in RequiemText by Manipal Digital Systems, Manipal
Printed at Thomson Press India Ltd, New Delhi

This book is sold subject to the condition that it shall not, by way of trade
or otherwise, be lent, resold, hired out, or otherwise circulated without the
publisher's prior consent in any form of binding or cover other than that in
which it is published and without a similar condition including this condition
being imposed on the subsequent purchaser.

www.penguin.co.in

Contents

Note on the Transliteration

For transliterating the original Persian text of the *masnavi Chiragh-e-Dair* I have focused on the sounds of the alphabet and therefore clubbed many of the common (or minutely varying) sounds represented by different letters together. The glossary for the transliteration follows.

Vowels:

a, as in b*u*t: ٰ
ā, as in f*a*r: آ, or consonant+ ا
i, as in t*í*p: ِ
ī, as in d*ee*p: ی
u, as in p*u*ll: ُ
ū, as in f*oo*l: consonant+ و
e, as in f*e*tch, written as -ey at word endings, unique to Indo-Persian accent: ے
-e-: represents the conjunction "of" in words with the *izāfat,* pronounced like the e above: ِ
o, as in g*oa*l: consonant+ و

Consonants:

b: ب

p: پ

t: ت، ط

s: ث،س،ص

j: ج

ch, as in chalk: چ

h: ح, ه

kh as in 'khan': خ

d as in 'dāl' or 'dil', a dental d sound: د

z: ض,ظ,ذ, ز

r: ر

sh: ش

'a, a guttural 'a': ع

gh, guttural g as in 'ghair' the other: غ

f: ف

q, a guttural k: ق

k: ک

g, as in girl, good: گ

l: ل

m: م

n: ن

ñ, nasal n, only partially pronounced: ں

w: و

y, for the sound of y as in young: ی

t, non-aspirated, dental t: ت

ḳh for aspirated k, specific to Urdu: کھ

T as in tool, specific to Urdu: ٹ

Introduction

Maaz Bin Bilal

hūñ garmī-e-nishāt-e-tasavvur se naghma sañj
maiñ andalīb-e-gulshan-e-nā-āfrīdah huñ[1]

I sing from the warmth of the joy of imagination
I am the bulbul of the garden not yet created

The garden has a prominent place as a sensuous image of fruition and abundance in Persianate poetry. It also works as a symbol for the ideal home/destination, reminiscent of paradise, tracing itself not just to the garden of Eden but also to a pre-Islamic legacy going back to ancient Iran. The term 'paradise' originated in the Avestan or Old Persian '*pairidaēza*' meaning 'enclosure, park'[2], originally the royal park or orchard of the king.[3] There is also the

---

[1] The verse is from one of Ghalib's many Urdu ghazals that he chose not to include in the belatedly published Urdu Diwan or collection of 1841.

[2] Etymology of paradise as given in OED.

[3] Julie Scott Meisami p. 231.

deeper allegory of the garden as the site for the Qur'anic injunction to read God's signs in nature.[4] In the above Urdu *sher* or distich, Ghalib appears to demand a new haven to sing his verse—not only in the spirit of *tāza goī* or 'fresh (poetry) telling' that had thrived in the Persianate poetry of the subcontinent since the sixteenth century but also for the sake of a more congenial political and cultural clime with appropriate recognition—a place of inner harmony, a home for his subtle sensibilities.

Mirza Asadullah Beg Khan, known more popularly by his *takhallus* or nom de plume 'Ghalib'[5] (1797–1869), was a modern poet who spent much of his life in quest of an audience receptive to his talents. In his early years his poetry was thought to be overtly complex and convoluted and in his later years the very court he sought patronage from was disbanded. A true poetic, spiritual, material, linguistic, and national home was either denied to him or placed in jeopardy for much of his lifespan. He was a poetic genius who worked across early colonial India's two major languages—Persian and Urdu—to aspire for a Hindustan that was either dying or was yet to come to fruition. Ghalib was, thus, among 'the last of the classicists and the first of the modernists'.[6] Altaf Husain Hali,[7] Ghalib's first

---

[4] Qur'an: 3:190: 'Behold! in the creation of the heavens and the earth, and the alternation of night and day, there are indeed signs for men of understanding' (Tr. Abdullah Yusuf Ali).

[5] Written as 'Ghalib' since that is how the popular poet is widely known although pronounced as Ghālib.

[6] Narang p. xix.

[7] Altaf Husain 'Hali' (1837–1914), poet, editor, critic, and biographer of Ghalib. Disciple of Shefta and Ghalib.

biographer has also argued that Persian poetry and prose in India saw its final heyday with Ghalib.

Ghalib lived his early life in times of political stability under the newly established *Pax Britannica* in Delhi after the decisive victory of General Gerald Lake, the British commander-in-chief, over the Marathas in 1803. Ghalib received a pension from the British on account of an uncle who had fought on their side. But, ironically, he sought cultural patronage from the Mughal court in the form of recognition for his poetry and formal titles. None of these was to last his lifetime. The post-Mutiny retributions[8] from the British resulted in the death of his brother and threatened his own life. The Mughal king Bahadur Shah Zafar honoured Ghalib as the royal *ustad* or tutor only after the death of his favourite poet, Ibrahim Zauq (1790–1854), whose poetry Ghalib considered inferior to his own. The honour came late, just a few years before the Revolt of 1857, following which the Mughal court was dismantled by the British, with Bahadur Shah sent to exile in 1858. Ghalib fought for his pension most of his life—sometimes for the correct amount and on other occasions just to be

---

[8] In 1857–58 there was a major rebellion by Indians against the British East India Company that ruled much of the subcontinent as a sovereign power. It began with the soldiers of the Meerut cantonment rebelling against the use of the animal-fat-greased bullet of the new Enfield rifles, but soon spread to many parts of the country. The rebelling soldiers arriving from Meerut to Delhi proclaimed the Mughal king Bahadur Shah Zafar as their leader. Subsequently, the British quelled what they called the soldier's mutiny and there were harsh retributions against anyone remotely linked to the insurgents, as the British swiftly won back all cities and territories they had lost in 1857–58.

paid. Daring to be wiser than his peers,[9] well aware of the moving cogs of modernity, and yet often impractically proud,[10] he was frequently out of place. Ghalib always remained a tenant on the move in Delhi. He was not only perpetually on the verge of residential dislocation as a man in debt but also in constant want of an ever-elusive multicultural and cosmopolitan home with suitable patronage for his intellectual sensibilities and abilities. During the long and arduous journey to the British capital of Calcutta[11] and back, between 1826 and 1829, the city struck him as the modern metropolis to covet. However, it was Banaras that came closest to the spiritual garden to which he wished to belong.[12] Subsequently, he endowed us with his only long poem written as a homage to a city. This famous poem written in Persian is *Chiragh-e-Dair,* which we may call *Temple Lamp.* It has been translated from Persian into English in its entirety here for the first time.[13]

---

[9] He understood the value of print early and rigorously saw his writings through the publishing process when most poetic culture was still oral. This has probably contributed to the establishment of Ghalib as a canonical poet since he was among the first to be prescribed across syllabi.

[10] e.g., he, on a matter of pride, refused a job at Delhi College that he desperately needed to settle his finances better.

[11] I use the older name 'Calcutta' (rather than 'Kolkata') in this volume as this is how it was known to Ghalib.

[12] Now officially known as Varanasi. I use Banaras, as Ghalib refers to the ancient city as 'Banaras' and 'Kashi' in the poem, which are also its contemporary common names.

[13] P.K. Nikhawan published a bridge translation in 2005 in Hindi and English, *Kaa'ba-e-Hindustan: Chirag-e-Dair,* translating from Kalidas Gupta Reza's Urdu translation of the original poem. This book is out of print and largely unavailable; even the publisher has closed down. Kuldip Salil

Albeit in his lifetime, and since, Ghalib has been primarily known as a ghazal poet, most famous for his Urdu ghazals, even though he wrote more in Persian. The next section, therefore, introduces the ghazal form, Ghalib as a ghazal poet, and mentions other genres that he wrote in, before giving way to more direct engagements with *Chiragh-e-Dair*.

2.1 Ghalib—the Ghazal Poet

> *kuchh to paDhiye keh log kahte haiñ*
> *aaj ghālib ghazal-sarā na huā*

> Please, do recite something, for people say,
> Ghalib's not recited a ghazal today.

The ghazal is a non-linear poem, usually of six to fourteen distiches, where each distich, *beit* in Persian and *sher* in Urdu, is a standalone independent verse and may have no narrative continuity with the rest of the poem. The word *'ghazal'* originates from the opening verses or *'taghazzul'* of the Arabic *qasīda* or ode. It literally means 'conversations with the beloved' although ghazals may have other themes than romance. It is also connected to the word *'ghazāl'*

---

has recently published a translation that has been accused of plagiarism and of being a bridge translation from Sadiq's Hindi translation of the poem without due acknowledgment. It retains Hindi words such as *'satnām'* and Sadiq's liberties with the original, taking it a little too far from the Persian, not just linguistically but also in the cultural implications of various concepts and meanings.

or 'gazelle' and its plaintive cry. Ghazals have an entire universe with some stock characters such as the *āshiq* (lover), *māshūq* (beloved), *raqīb* (rival), *sāqi* (wine pourer), *rind* (drunk), *sheikh* (saint), *wāiz* (preacher), *shāhid* (witness), *zāhid* (abstinent), Sufi and so on. Each ghazal is held together by its mood and a regular poetic metre, which the poet sets in the first *beit* or *sher*, which is called *matlā*. The *matlā* also carries a refrain or *radīf* at the end of both hemistiches and rhymes or *qāfiya* that precede the *radīf* in both lines. This rhyme and refrain pattern is repeated in the second line of every subsequent verse, so each *sher* or *beit* has a sense of foreknowledge about its end, and yet retains a sense of wonder as to how the poet would get to it in each verse. Each *beit* is further an exposition or question in the first line which gets a witty response in the second, almost in the sense of an elaborate metaphor such as the metaphysical conceit. The final distich is *maqtā,* which has the poet's *takhallus,* and forces the poet to often address himself in third person or to create witty puns on their own names. Not only does this usage of the penname create quite the unique effect of a poetic stance that is extremely humble or arrogant, or disingenuously both, but it also becomes an embedded mark of authorship in a largely oral culture.

The almost incantatory, rhythmic prosody of the ghazal has made it the most popular form of the mushaira or the public poetic symposia, which used to be more private in Ghalib's time. Most often they were held at the court or at the homes of the elite. Today, mushairas are most often large public events where the poets read from a mic on a stage, addressing gatherings that may run into many thousands. Ghalib certainly made a mark at the mushairas of his time although he had a number of contemporaries, friends and rivals who were excellent poets themselves, such as Momin Khan Momin (1800–1852), Sheikh Ibrahim Zauq (1790–1854), Mufti Sadruddin Aazurdah (1804–1868), Imaam Bakhsh Sehbaai (c.1806–1857), Nawab Mustafa Khan Shefta (1809–1869), and Dagh Dehlavi (1831–1905). The king Bahadur Shah Zafar was a commendable poet himself.

Ghalib certainly wrote a lot of love poetry involving the stock figures of the ghazal universe described above which has withstood the test of time. But he is also known for invoking deep pathos, existential angst, spirituality, devotion, and religious skepticism and for questioning orthodoxy—sometimes through an emphasis on wine drinking, which always carried the double edge of Sufi divine inspiration. Another important theme running through most of his ghazals is his most strong belief in his own ability as a poet and therefore the superiority of his vision of the world. I give below an Urdu ghazal by Ghalib both to further explain the ghazal itself and to showcase Ghalib's mastery of the form.

bāzicha-e-atfāl hai duniyā mere āge
hotā hai shab-o-roz tamāshā mere āge

ik khel hai aurañg-e-sulaimāñ mere nazdīk
ik baat hai ejāz-e-masīhā mere āge

juz naam nahīñ sūrat-e-ālam mujhe manzūr
juz vahm nahīñ hastī-e-ashiyā mere āge

hotā hai nihāñ gard meñ sahrā mere hote
ghistā hai jabīñ khaak pe dariyā mere āge

mat pūchh ki kyā haal hai merā tere pīchhe
tū dekh ki kyā rañg hai terā mere āge

sach kahte ho khud-bīn o khud-ārā hūñ na kyūñ hūñ
baiThā hai but-e-ā.ina-sīmā mere āge

phir dekhiye andāz-e-gul-afshānī-e-guftār
rakh de koī paimāna-e-sahbā mere āge

nafrat kā gumāñ guzre hai maiñ rashk se guzrā
kyūñkar kahūñ lo naam na un kā mere āge

īmāñ mujhe roke hai jo khīñche hai mujhe kufr
ka'aba mere pīchhe hai kalīsā mere āge

āshiq hūñ pa māshūq-farebī hai mirā kaam
majnūñ ko burā kahtī hai lailā mere āge

khush hote haiñ par vasl meñ yūñ mar nahīñ jaate
aa.ī shab-e-hijrāñ kī tamannā mere āge

hai maujzan ik qulzum-e-khūñ kaash yahī ho
aatā hai abhī dekhiye kyā kyā mere āge

go haath ko jumbish nahīñ āñkhoñ meñ to dam hai
rahne do abhī sāghar -o-mīnā mere āge

ham-pesha o ham-mashrab o hamrāz hai merā
'ghālib' ko burā kyūñ kaho achchhā mere āge

My English translation:

A child's play is the world in front of me
Night and day, the tamasha is swirled in front of me.

A game is the throne of Solomon to me,
The miracle of the Messiah too is told in front of me.

Not more than as a name do I accept this globe's mien,
A legend is the being of the world in front of me.

The desert's hidden with dust in my presence,
In dirt, the river's forehead is rubbed in front of me.

Don't ask of my condition in your absence,
You look at what colours you're pearled in, in front of me.

The doubts of hatred pass, I have passed through envy,
Why'd I say, don't let their name be called in front of me?

You speak truth that I am vain and arrogant too,
Behold there sits the silver-mirrored idol in front of me.

Look at the flow of words, my delivery's command,
If only you kept a glass of wine cuddled in front of me.

Faith stops me as sin draws me out,
The Kaaba is behind, a cathedral in front of me.

Since I am a lover, my profession is to cheat,
Laila calls Majnūñ a scoundrel in front of me.

We're happy at the union but we don't really die,
A hope for separation has rolled in front of me.

If only that tumultuous river of blood were this,
Let's see now what all is whirled in front of me.

If the hand has no reach, the eyes still see,
Let the bottle and glass be settled in front of me.

My colleague, my fellow drinker, my secret-keeper—he is,
Why call Ghalib bad?—he's of a better world, in front
of me.[14]

As should be evident above, not only has Ghalib mastered
the prosodic elements of the ghazal, but this ghazal, which
is one of his most famous ones, is also the perfect example
of the plethora of themes at play in his work. 'Mere āge' or
'in front of me' is the refrain or the *radīf*. This is preceded
by the rhyme or the *qāfiya* of 'ā' as in *'duniyā'* and *'tamashā'*

---

[14] First published in *Indiana Review*.

of both the lines of the first distich or the matlā and the second line of every subsequent *sher*. I have only partially managed to recreate the *qāfiya* among the 'whirled', 'settled', 'world', 'told', 'swirled' slant rhymes. The metre of the original Urdu ghazal is *hazaj musamman akhrab makfūf mahzūf*.[15] The themes move from the marked superiority of Ghalib's vision and creation to that of nature, a firm belief in his poetic abilities, the games that lovers play, wine-drinking, which is taboo in Islam and so acquires a radical, heterodox edge here, and a claim to be a Sufi dervish in his divine wisdom in the *maqta* or the final verse. Even more strongly, perhaps, the poem also shows Ghalib's trademark restlessness and sense of dissatisfaction with the world.

But what is less widely known perhaps is that Ghalib wrote in other poetic forms and even prose. In his later life, he collected and published the letters he had written, over many years, in Urdu to friends. Through their publication, he seems to have sought to establish a (natural) conversational style of Urdu prose over the florid and formal (artificial) style that had so far prevailed. He seems to have succeeded in this since, like his poetry, his letters were among the early Urdu writing to be published and to be prescribed in academic curricula and continue to remain there.

Ghalib also wrote *qasīda* or odes (although he is on record expressing his disdain for them) in praise of different nobles, the Mughal king, and important British officials, both in Persian and Urdu. He wrote *qatā* too, which are monothematic verses most often of four-

---

[15] Sagheer-un-Nisa Begum. p.412.

lines. He even started writing a history for the Mughal king, although he did not get very far with it. Ghalib did write strong criticism, volumes such as the *Qati-e-Burhān*, indirectly defending his own poetics, while deriding other masters. He also published a diary in Persian, *Dastañbuy*, following the mutiny retributions of 1858, largely in praise of the British, probably to prevent himself from meeting the same fate of a beheading or exile as faced by his friends and acquaintances from the Mughal court and his wider circles. Finally, and for our purposes in this volume, he wrote eleven *masnavis* or long narrative poems in Persian, one of which is our concern here.[16]

It was ghazals that won Ghalib and his writing much renown, but the poetic respite and fulfillment he always yearned for are most evidently realized in his long poem, *Chirāgh-e-Dair*, which he wrote in Banaras, a city that seems to have been an ephemeral haven for him.

2.2 The Banaras Sojourn: Context

Ghalib was a man proud of his Indo-Turkish lineage and poetic prowess in Urdu and Persian. Besides writing poetry, honing his poetic craft, and undertaking affiliated labour, he seems to have wanted to do no other work throughout his life of seventy odd years. He liked to live well, drinking Old Tom whisky[17] that he would purchase

---

[16] The form of the *masnavi* is explained in much detail later under the section *Temple Lamp: Poetics*.

[17] There is speculation that Old Tom could be a gin, like the contemporary drink with this brand name, although Ghalib's Old Tom was a dark-

from the Meerut cantonment, and maintained a retinue of servants. This lifestyle could not have been supported merely by his poetry, which could at best be patronized by a vassal ruler such as the Mughal king Bahadur Shah Zafar II or other nawabs such as those of Rampur or Awadh. The pension (as he called it) that he received from the British was the premise of such a lifestyle. Difficulties in obtaining his pension in full led Ghalib to petition the British. His arduous journey on foot, horseback, bullock cart, and boat from Delhi all the way to the capital at Calcutta, roughly a distance of 1,500 kilometres, took him over a year as he repeatedly fell ill. He stopped en route in Banaras, where he found physical and spiritual healing.

Ghalib's father, Abdullah Beg Khan, a soldier, died in 1801 or 1802 in the service of the Maharaja of Alwar when Ghalib was only four or five years old. His uncle, Nasrullah Beg Khan, also a soldier, assumed the guardianship for Ghalib and his younger brother, Yusuf Mirza. Nasrullah Beg Khan had married the sister of Nawab Ahmad Bakhsh Khan, and the brothers-in-law had fought together against the Marathas for Lord Lake, the commander-in-chief of the British Army in India, in his successful campaigns of 1802–3. The Nawab was rewarded for his efforts with a *jagir* (estate) in Ferozpur-Jhirka by Commander Lake as well as the pargana of Loharu by the Maharaja of Alwar. Nasrullah Beg was granted a permanent *jāgir* with an income of one lakh rupees by Commander Lake. But, unfortunately,

---

coloured liquor. It could have even been rum. Ghalib has mentioned in his correspondence that he encountered gin in Banaras.

Nasrullah Beg also died—falling off an elephant—when Ghalib was still quite young, only nine years old.

The British confiscated the *jāgīr* upon Beg's death, but Nawab Ahmed Bakhsh Khan negotiated a stipend in lieu of it in the name of Nasrullah Beg's dependents. A sum of 25,000 rupees was to be deducted from Bakhsh Khan's annual taxes due to the government, and he was to provide 10,000 rupees as annual stipend to Nasrullah Beg Khan's dependents and to use 15,000 rupees to maintain Nasrullah Beg's 400-strong cavalry to be provided to the British on demand. Khwaja Haji, a distant relative and employee of Nasrullah Beg, who brought the cavalry to the Nawab, managed to ingratiate himself and obtain a part of the legacy of the dependents of Nasrullah Beg. The avaricious Nawab managed to retain for himself half of the money intended for the dependents. Thus, the final settlement of family pensions was: 5,000 rupees for the Nawab, 2,000 rupees for Khwaja Haji (commander of the horsemen, even though the British had allowed a separate waiver of 15,000 rupees of tax towards the maintenance of the cavalry), 1,500 rupees for the mother and sisters of Nasrullah Beg, and 1,500 rupees for Mirza Ghalib and Yusuf Mirza, the only male heirs.

Ghalib was too young at the award of the stipends to fully understand the injustice being done to his brother, Yusuf, and him. He later became aware of how he had been robbed of a large share of the inheritance belonging to him and his family by the Nawab and Khwaja Haji. Ghalib grew discontented over the corruption and eventually decided to appeal to the British authorities. At first, he did not recognize the Nawab's hand behind this miscarriage of justice and tried to seek his help in a redressal. He had become further related to the Nawab by getting married to his brother Mirza Ilahi Bakhsh's daughter, Umrao Begum. The Nawab promised Ghalib that Khwaja Haji's share would be suspended upon his death, but it was in fact transferred to his children upon Haji's demise in 1825. By this time, the elder Nawab had been succeeded by his son Nawab Shamsuddin Ahmad Khan[18]. Ghalib visited the elder Nawab many times at Ferozpur Jhirka to convince him of his rightful demands only to be told that nothing could be done without the permission of the British Resident. It was ostensibly for this purpose that the Nawab took Ghalib along with him to Bharatpur to meet Lord Metcalfe, though he did not actually introduce him. Following this disappointment, Ghalib stayed on in Ferozpur-Jhirka till January 1826. In this period, he made up his mind to meet the British Resident on his own, without the Nawab's intercession.

Heavily in debt by this time and trying to avoid his creditors in Delhi, it is unclear if he visited Delhi in secret or not, but Ghalib then headed to Kanpur to meet Lord Metcalfe. Ghalib reached Kanpur via Farukhabad but fell very ill and had to be carried across the river to Lucknow to seek medical treatment. The plan to meet the Resident failed. Ghalib recuperated in Lucknow

---

[18] Who would be later hanged by the British for hiring one Kureem Khan to murder Delhi's then British Resident, William Fraser, who was an admirer of Ghalib and whom the latter considered an ally.

for five months, and in this time, he tried to obtain the patronage of the Nawab of Awadh, Ghaziuddin Haider. He even wrote a *qasīda* or ode in the honour of the Nawab, but he also set strict conditions for his reception by the Nawab, which were not accepted. The meeting with the Nawab never took place. Ghalib's keen sense of honour as a poet and his pride as a member of the Turko-Indian elite often got in his way during his life, and this was another such instance.[19]

Ghalib changed his plans and decided to continue westward and to go to Calcutta to petition the Governor General himself. For this, he first went to Banda, where he had a wealthy cousin. He fell ill here again and stayed another six months. He also befriended the *sadr-e-amin* or the civil magistrate, Nawab Muhammad Ali Khan, a notable poet of his time (we shall look at one of the letters Ghalib wrote to him from Banaras about the city, below). Khan helped to finance the rest of Ghalib's trip to Calcutta.

Next, Ghalib reached Allahabad via Chilla Tara, hoping to stay there for some days, but fled the city, possibly on account of some disputes with a fan of the Indo-Persian poet, Qatīl, whose work he despised. He took the boat from Allahabad and reached Banaras. In the often-quoted

---

[19] Similarly, Ghalib gave up an appointment as a professor at Delhi College in 1840, as he returned home after waiting in vain on his first day at the college gate for the college principal to come and personally receive him. The principal refused to discriminate between college employees, and could not oblige Ghalib. The latter believed that as a renowned poet and a visitor to the court, a college job should only enhance the honours due to him, not reduce them. The impasse could not be broken. Ghalib never took up the job though he had desperately needed the income.

Persian letter to Nawab Muhammad Ali Khan, Ghalib writes disparagingly of Allahabad, and fondly of reaching Banaras:

What a ridiculous place is Ilahabad[20]! May God get rid of it; for it has no healing for the sick, nor anything of note for the gentleman. Neither do men and women have any life here, nor do its young and old have any love or kindness in their hearts. Its people are a blot on the face of this earth. Its desolate inhabitation is only worth tilling as farmland . . . It is unfair to call this terrible valley a city, and it is so shameful that a person should stay in this dwelling of ghosts . . . Because it has heard that the sinful would also obtain grace for the sake of the virtuous, it has cast its hundred thousand dishonours with its three thousand hopes with the lot of Banaras, and sent the river Ganges speeding towards Banaras as a sign of respect.

However much of a burden Banaras may find it to look at this black-faced city, its heart is comforted by the knowledge that the Ganga lies between the two. By God, if the return journey from Calcutta means that I have to travel through Ilahabad, then I shall drop the very idea of returning home and never return. Suffice it to say, after spending a night and day in this city of ghosts for the crime of not having had my luggage delivered yet,

[20] The British called the city Allahabad, and it was recently renamed officially in India as Prayagraj. It is pronounced and written in Urdu and Hindi as Ilahabad, the land of ilahi or god(s). Akbar is supposed to have founded the city and called it Ilahabas.

I found a ride the next morning, and quickly reached the banks of the Jamuna. I crossed the river like a fast gust of wind and made my way to Banaras.[21]

Ghalib's health recovered immediately upon arrival here. He rejoiced in the pleasant breeze and the verdant environs of the holy city and stayed in Banaras for a month before leaving for Calcutta, even though he had intended to stay here only a few days. He writes fondly of the city of light and recounts his humble living arrangements in the same letter to Nawab Muhammad Ali Khan of Banda:

> On Thursday, a heavenly, life-affirming breeze arose from the east that energized me and refreshed my soul. The miracle of this breeze cleared the haze I was enveloped in and lifted my spirits like victory banners. The waves of the cool breeze swept away all weakness from my body.
>
> What can I say about the city of Banaras! It would be justified if I were to call it the mark on the heart of the universe because of its excessively heart-warming qualities.[22] And what do I say about the surroundings of

---

[21] Translated from the Urdu translation of the original Persian letter quoted in Yaqoob Yawar's essay, 'Ghalib, Banaras, aur Masnavi *Chiragh-e-Dair*'.

[22] 'the mark on the heart': '*suvaida*' in the original text. A more literal translation would be to call Banaras 'a *black spot* on the heart of the universe', with various possible interpretations. It could imply that Banaras is the black mark to ward off the evil eye or could even be a reference to the Quranic verse that says God created man from a clot of blood. It was also traditionally believed that there was a dark spot in the

this settlement? It would be proper to call it heaven on earth because of the foliage and flowers that are in bloom in their full glory. Its breeze blows life into dead bodies. Its every fleck of dust has the qualities to pull thorns and needles away like magnets from the feet of travellers. The river Ganga would not have been considered so noble had it not rubbed its forehead at its feet. And if the sun had not shone over the walls and gates of this city, it would not have been this bright and radiant. The flow of the Ganga sounds like that of a storm. The banks of the Ganga are home to the most learned of men. With the reflections of the homes of the angel-faced beautiful ladies in the green waters, the homes of the pious have shattered like the *Katāñ* cloth.[23] If I were to describe the buildings of this city, then they are the abodes of the intoxicated, and the flowers and vegetation of the surroundings suggest that this is the land of perpetual spring.

Following upon these rapturous praises of the city in prose to his friend, it was here in this garden city of perpetual

---

middle of the heart. Furthermore, the black spot is supposed to occur more specifically on the heart of a doe out of grief, when its fawn has been killed. Perhaps, Ghalib is either referring to the great importance Banaras has as the emotional centre of the heart of the universe, or this could even be a reference to the many deaths and death rites that occur on the city's banks. Finally, in Sufism, '*suvaida*' is believed to be the sixth portion of the heart, the home of knowledge and revelation.

[23] The katāñ cloth is supposed to be so delicate that it is shredded by moonlight.

spring that Ghalib wrote, in Persian, arguably his most famous and best *masnavi*,[24] *Temple Lamp*.

He also recounts that he first stayed in a *sarai* or tavern for a week and then rented the small house of an old woman in the Aurangabad area (although Ghalib writes it mistakenly as 'Naurangabad'). In modern Banaras, the locality is close to Dalmandi, the abode of courtesans in his time, not far from one of the chief ghats, Dashashvamedha, where one can imagine Ghalib witnessing the *arti* rituals and seeing the sun rise from the opposite bank of the Ganga.

The Banaras Ghalib visited was a city of peace. The ruling empire was of vassal kings who held sway under the aegis of the East India Company. Raja Udit Narain Singh held power when Ghalib arrived in late 1826. The ghats and most of the newer temples had been constructed mostly under the patronage of the Marathas, with the decline of the Mughals in the previous century.

During this stay, Ghalib did not meet anyone of note, though Banaras had enough personages, both poets and royals, whom a person of Ghalib's stature would have been expected to make contact with. One wonders why. Some answers may be offered in the poem itself. But before we analyze the text of *Temple Lamp*, we must first examine the context of the historical and cultural discourse about Banaras, and the place of *Temple Lamp* in Ghalib's body of work.

---

[24] Explained in more detail in the section *Temple Lamp: Poetics*.

2.3 The Lamp of Banaras: Discursive Location and Critical Reception

Banaras today is often a metonym for India. The popular discourse on the city traces its antiquity from Puranic sources such as the *Kāshī Khanda*,[25] *Kāshī Rahasya*[26], and the *Kāshī Māhātmaya*.[27] From colonial Orientalists such as James Prinsep (1799–1840) to contemporary scholars such as Diana L. Eck (b. 1945), writers in English go to Sanskrit sources for myths and legends and to pandits and Hindu pilgrims for lived testimonies to describe this foremost of Hindu pilgrimage sites. Banaras signifies the abode of Shiva, a place for moksha, of temples, ghats, and the holy Ganga—the city of light.

One hardly ever comes across Persian sources when reading popular discourse on Banaras, even though Persian was a hegemonic language in India for close to a thousand years.[28] More than a quarter of the city's

---

[25] The *Kāshī Khanda* is one of the seven khandas or parts of the thirteenth Purana, *Skanda Purana*. It has more than 13,000 slokas or couplets. It is a narration on Kashi (Banaras) by Lord Skanda (Shiva's son, also known as Karitkeya or Murugan). This is framed by the further narration of Sage Vyasa. It acquired its present written form probably in the fourteenth century. See Eck for more details p.347.

[26] A mystical text in twenty-six chapters that identifies the city with Brahman, the universal creative spirit, dating from the fourteenth to the seventeenth century. See Eck p.347 for more details.

[27] A *māhātmaya* is praise literature. *Kāshī Māhātmaya* dates from the fourteenth to the seventeenth century and is composed of thirty-one chapters. See Eck for more details p.347.

[28] Refer to Richard Eaton on the Persian Cosmopolis, the period from 900–1900 CE when Persian was the cosmopolitan language in India, irrespective of religion.

population comprises Muslims,[29] but their testimonies are rarely solicited to understand the city.[30] While popular imagination accepts numerous Hindu temples and deities of the city as its hallmarks, it glosses over the one thousand Muslim shrines and mosques to be found in the city. The academic Madhuri Desai has pointed out: 'colonial representations of the city simultaneously rendered it static and Hindu' (29).[31] The ghats, which were largely built in the eighteenth century by the Marathas and Rajputs, are commonly looked upon as ancient structures, their strong Mughal architectural influence rendered invisible. When Prinsep, Eck, or other contemporary commentators in the popular discourse refer to Muslims or the Mughal realm to which Ghalib belonged, they are seen as antagonistic to Banaras. They are portrayed as aggressors who destroyed temples or subjugated the city. On the other hand, destruction of heritage temples is acceptable today when projected as part of 'development', even though it may result in displacements, loss of heritage, and resentments. The grants by Sultanate or Mughal emperors to various

---

[29] James Prinsep conducted a survey of Banaras in 1828–29, where he found 121,446 Hindus and 31,248 Muslims in the city (*Benares Illustrated* 14). The 2011 census records the demographics as follows:
   Hindus: 840,280 (70.11 per cent) and Muslims: 345,461 (28.82 per cent).

[30] Only certain anthropological works take the Muslim weavers of the famous Banarasi silk into account or try to counter Eck's claims of the Hindu sacred geography of Banaras. Refer to the works of Ciotti, Kumar, and Williams for example.

[31] Rendering the Orient as static is a classical trope in Orientalist discourse as has been pointed out by Edward Said.

temple trusts or the contributions to the city of various Muslims or those belonging to the Persosphere are rarely acknowledged.[32]

It is to view the city also through a Persian cultural inheritance, from the perspective of arguably the best poet of the nineteenth century, from the perspective of a Hindustani Muslim, that one must read Ghalib's *Chiragh-e-Dair*, his *Temple Lamp*.[33] The poem gives us many remarkable insights into the city's spirituality and ecology, into its natural and physical beauty, and primarily that of its people, in the early nineteenth century. Ghalib acquaints us with the pride of place Banaras has as a world religious site, a social locus of Hindustan, and as a centre in the global Persosphere extending from Turkey to Bengal and across the Silk Route. Thus, it is to question the inward-looking discourse around Banaras, premised only on Sanskritic traditions, that one must study *Temple Lamp* as a major discursive and cultural intervention. It allows us a glimpse of Banaras as it existed for people other than pandits, pilgrims, and colonial scholars for almost a thousand years.

---

[32] In fact, Prinsep at least acknowledges the destruction of the city of Banaras over the battle for supremacy between Vaishnavites and Shaivites (9), whereas Eck's attitude towards the Hindus of Banaras only indicates them to be pious and constructive towards Banaras and almost all Muslims to be only destructive.

[33] Following the work of Manan Ahmed, *The Loss of Hindustan*, it is important to recognize Ghalib as a colonized man whose conception of India was evolving from the thousand-year-old Hindustan to the colonized India, which was to be enforced fully after 1857. It is this colonized India that gave birth to the independent Indian state with its colonial residues and outlooks.

There has been a rich prior tradition of writing in Persian on Banaras, which I hope this work also leads readers to pursue. Sheikh Ali Hazin Lahiji, for example, was an Iranian who came to Banaras c. 1750 and lies buried there today with a shrine dedicated to him. He was a poet who wrote in praise of the city:

> *az banāras na rawam ma'abad-e-'aam ast īñjā*
> *har brahman-e-pisar-e-lachhman-o-rām ast īñjā*

I will not leave Banaras for it is holy everywhere,
Every Brahman here is a son of Lachhman or Ram.[34]

In Mirza Ghalib's own oeuvre, the prominence of his Urdu writing has overshadowed the importance of his Persian writings to such an extent that the majority of readers are hardly aware of the latter. Yet the bulk of his work was written in Persian. While there have been innumerable translations of his Urdu verses, very little of his Persian poetry has been translated into English. This is the first complete English translation of his famous *masnavi Chiragh-e-Dair* directly from the Persian original. It is important for a fuller and wider understanding of Mirza Ghalib's body of work that there are more translations of his Persian work, just as there exist those of his Urdu corpus, and I hope

---

[34] The concern here is of course elitist in terms of caste, as is Ghalib's in *Temple Lamp*. Both Hazin and Ghalib belonged to the community of Indian elite in the Persosphere, whose peers in the public sphere were primarily upper-caste Hindus, besides the Turko-Mughal and other *shurfaa*, the Muslim elite.

this humble offering shall serve as an added stimulus. Mehr Afshan Farooqi's recent monograph *Ghalib: A Wilderness at my Doorstep* provides an astute appraisal of Ghalib's poetry and reception with a view to the chronological editions of both his Persian and Urdu writing.

Ghalib himself often prioritized his Persian compositions over his Urdu works. Even his Urdu poetry was far more complex and Persianized than that of his contemporaries or predecessors. He was proud of tracing a *Sabk-e-Hindi* or Indo-Persian poetic influence on his Urdu poetry,[35] as the following Urdu *sher* on his idol, Bedil, hailed

---

[35] Rajeev Kinra has argued in his essay 'Fresh Words for a Fresh World: Tāza-Gū'ī and the Poetics of Newness in Early Modern Indo-Persian Poetry' that the term early Mughal poets used for their poetry was '*tāza-gū'ī*' or 'speaking the fresh'. '*Sabk-e-Hindi*', he explains, is most probably a pejorative term created by the Iranian poet laureate and scholar, Muhammad Taqī Bahār, in the early twentieth century as he was trying to argue for a superior classical Persian and created subsequent periodization of Persian literary history named after the main centres of patronage in each period. The Mughal court in its heyday being the most suitable patron for Persian poets therefore gave the name *Sabk-e-Hindi* to its age and to all the poetry of the Persosphere, not just that of the subcontinent. However, I use '*Sabk-e-Hindi*' in a colloquial sense to refer to the Indo-Persian dialect, culture, literature, accent, and unique orthography, as most contemporary South-Asian academics, scholars, and writers working with Persian do as a handy term for the Persian of South Asia. It may have not been available to Chandar Bhān Brahman, the great poet writing in Persian at Shahjehan's court, as Kinra argues, and possibly not even to Ghalib. But Ghalib did share an anxiety about the value of Indo-Persian poetry when compared to that of Iran, which is also Bahār's argument. Moreover, we use a term such as 'Urdu' for the works of the major poets of the tradition such as Mir Taqi Mir, whereas hardly anyone knew the term up to the eighteenth century, and even Ghalib in the nineteenth disliked the word 'Urdu', and he called his own language 'Hindi', 'Hindvi' or 'Rekhta'. 'Hind', 'Hindu', 'India'

as one of the foremost poets of the Indo-Persian tradition, suggests:

tarz-e-bedil meñ reḳhta kahnā
asadullāh khāñ qayāmat hai

Writing Rekhta in the manner of Bedil,
By God, Asadullah Khan, what a feat!

However, his relationship with Bedil was to become more complex over time as we shall soon see.

Ghalib wrote Urdu poetry from a young age but turned to Persian in the mature phase of his life. *Temple Lamp* is his third *masnavi* and lies at the cusp of his shift from Urdu to Persian. He wrote this *masnavi* probably in Banaras in 1826, as he was en route to Calcutta or after reaching the metropolis. Upon arrival in Calcutta, he found an alternative, in some ways a more powerful, resonant Persosphere than Delhi in the eastern colonial metropolis, where there were ambassadors present from Iran, and both the Bengalis and the British were also writing and publishing widely in Persian. Ghalib probably wished to communicate with a wider audience, even beyond India, than Urdu could allow. Writing in Persian, he could draw upon the better-established traditions of Persian aesthetics rather than having to create the more complex innovations

---

are also terms first given by Persians, Arabs, and Europeans that are now accepted and used by Indians to refer to themselves.

he brought to Urdu poetry. And so, he told his readers in his Persian collection:

> *fārsī bīn tāb bīnī naqshhāi rañg rañg*
> *biguzar az majmu'ah-e-urdū keh berañg-e-manast*

Read my Persian verses to behold pictures of varied hues,
Overlook the Urdu collection, for it is colourless.[36]

Yet, finding acceptability for his Persian verse in Calcutta was a tall task at first. Khwaja Haji, who was the controversial recipient of a part of Ghalib's pension, had arrived in Calcutta before him and done his best to sully Ghalib's reputation. Not only had he cast doubt on

---

[36] The second line literally reads as 'my colourless' in the original. The Indo-Persian scholar, Prashant Keshavmurthy, has alerted me to how this may be a reference 'from Mughal courtly painting practice where it refers to the 'cartoon' or colourless charcoal tracing which formed the blueprint or basis for what might or might not be filled in with colour. In Persian courtly painting, in contrast to Renaissance European visual culture, drawing was privileged over painting. Hence the Greek/ Byzantine (i.e., Sufi) victory over the Chinese (i.e., philosopher-engineer) in Rumi's account of the painting competition in his *Masnavi*. Given this technical sense (which [one] will also find in Bedil's ghazals), Ghalib's verse could be construed as saying that his Urdu ghazals are the Platonic basis of his colourful Persian collection, that his Urdu poetry is of an ontologically higher grade than his Persian.' Nonetheless, despite this counterargument, the more voluminous and more colourful Persian poetry of Ghalib as compared to his Urdu verse cannot be ignored or taken to be of any less value. In fact, conventional wisdom in Ghalib studies does suggest that Ghalib prioritized his Persian poetry more as written in the classical language of Persian as opposed to the modern language of Hindi or Rekhta, which later came to be known as Urdu.

Ghalib's authorship of his poems, by citing the earlier penname of Asad, but thereby creating confusion, he even spread a rumour that Ghalib had badmouthed Qatīl, the popular poet of Calcutta. Qatīl's fans took up arms against Ghalib. They said Ghalib's style and diction was breaking away from tradition and accepted usage. Qatīl's fans berated Ghalib publicly and his friends even feared for personal harm to the poet. As a response, Ghalib wrote another *masnavi*, *Bād-i-Mukhālif* or *The Contrary Wind*, which was ostensibly a poetic treatise. However, while Ghalib claimed that it was a reconciliatory overture, he had in fact belittled all Indo-Persian or *Sabk-e-Hindi* poetry here, except for Bedil, and also mock-praised Qatīl, before ending with the mention of Qatīl's inability to write good Persian.[37] Thus, while the poem was written to discredit Qatīl and establish himself as a Persian poet outside the Indo-Persian tradition, Ghalib was throwing the baby out with the bathwater. Proceeding with this (flawed) logic in later life, he had to even discredit his favourite Indo-Persian poet, Bedil.[38] He even claimed (probably falsely) to have studied as a child under the tutelage of an Iranian tutor in Agra, Abdus Samad, who was, in all likelihood, a figment of Ghalib's imagination. Ghalib asserted that this native knowledge of Persian was the reason for his superior verse as opposed to his Indian peers. Ghalib made

---

[37] Farooqi, 103–6.

[38] In a letter to Abdul Ghafur Sarwar in 1859, Ghalib wrote: 'Nasir Ali and Bedil and Ghanimat—of what worth is their Persian? . . . Their poetry doesn't have that taste, it doesn't have that style of Iranians.' (Faruqi, 17; Farooqi, 108).

this claim about his Iranian tutor in the critical text, *Qati-e-Burhan*, which he wrote after the Mutiny reprisals of 1858 when he was restricted to his home, and most of his friends and family had been killed or forced into exile from Delhi. The volume critiques an Indo-Persian dictionary *Burhān-e-Qati*, where Ghalib disparages the author and Indo-Persian scholarship in general. This created further furore and drew retaliatory criticism from the contemporary Indo-Persian literati.[39]

Ghalib's self-created quagmire of an inferiority in Indo-Persian verse as opposed to Iranian verse was symptomatic of a larger inferiority complex as well. Shamsur Rehman Faruqi (1935–2020), the recently deceased maverick author, critic, editor, and historian, tells us in his essay *'Mutalla'at-e-Ghalib, Sabk-e-Hindi, aur Pairvi Maghribi'* that this feeling wavered over time.[40] The eighteenth century had seen the best of Persian poetry by Indians, as they still retained a great confidence in their unique Indo-Persian linguistic and poetic abilities. The nineteenth century, with the British replacing Persian with English and the vernaculars as official languages in India, saw tremendous anxiety among the Indo-Persian literati regarding the place of their language and literature vis-à-vis the global Persosphere. Ghalib, who was struggling to find a place in the Sabk-e-Hindi tradition, hit out at the whole Indo-Persian canon and exacerbated its sense of decline and lack of self-worth, while trying to establish his

---

[39] Farooqi, 20–4.
[40] Faruqi, 9–38.

own. From 1828, when he was in Calcutta, till his death in 1869, Ghalib orchestrated a campaign, with the support of peers such as Shefta[41] and disciples such as Hali,[42] against the *Sabk-e-Hindi* or Indo-Persian literary tradition.[43]

The question of reception or gaining repute for his Persian poetry within the Indo-Persian literary culture of the nineteenth century became somewhat moot as the whole tradition was being denigrated by the author, and it appears the Indo-Persian literati by this time was starting to suffer from an inferiority complex. Continuing in Ghalib's own tradition of snubbing the Indo-Persian poets, Shibli Nomani (1857–1914), the Islamic and literary scholar of note, included neither Bedil nor Ghalib in his foundational volume of literary history, *Sher-ul-Ajam* or *The Poetry of Persian*. Still, Ghalib is, of course, a leading name within the tradition of Indo-Persian poetry however much he hit out against it. Yet, it is once Ghalib began to be compared as a poet across literary traditions in a comparative framework by different critics that he made his strongest mark leading to his global reputation.

Altaf Husain Hali (1837–1914), Ghalib's disciple and biographer, who published *Yadgar-e-Ghalib* or *Memorial to*

---

[41] Nawab Mustafa Khan 'Shefta' (1806–1869), a nawab with an estate in Palwal, Gurgaon; Ghalib's friend and contemporary; poet in Urdu and Farsi; used the *takhallus* or pennames 'Shefta' and 'Hasrati' in the two languages respectively.

[42] Hali also argued after the 1857 mutiny suppressions and the subsequent abject defeat of Mughal culture for modern, narrative, and naturalistic Urdu poetry going beyond the traditional Persian-Urdu classicism and romantic, spiritual, and metaphysical poetry.

[43] Faruqi, p. 19.

Ghalib in 1897, may be said to have begun this tradition of extricating Ghalib from the limitations of comparisons just to Iranian literature, putting him instead at par with Western writers. Hali praised Ghalib for the truth and passion of his verse (qualities we find in great abundance in *Temple Lamp*) as opposed to the artificiality and hyperbole of traditional Urdu-Persian poetry. For Hali, Ghalib was deeply aware of the Persian-Urdu traditions, but not bound by them; Ghalib could easily stand up to the poets of the West.[44] Not long after Hali, Abdur Rahman Bijnori (1885–1918), a brilliant litterateur, who unfortunately died young, offered the highest praise to Ghalib when he stated in his introduction to Ghalib's verse published in 1921 that India has produced two texts of divine revelation, the sacred Vedas and Ghalib's collection of verse. He further 'claimed that Ghalib's ideas on existence, reality, nature, and the endlessness of imagination resonated in Goethe's poetry' and also compared him to Kant, Nietzsche, Hegel, Spencer, Rimbaud, and other European writers.[45] This properly started a tradition of regarding Ghalib as a world poet. Shamsur Rehman Faruqi astutely recognizes how this further removed Ghalib from comparisons to Indo-Persian greats such as Bedil and Urfi and considered him at par with Wordsworth and Shakespeare, which meant that Ghalib was now read like a Western poet, even by Indians (25).

---

[44] Faruqi, pp. 22–3.
[45] Farooqi, p. 39.

There has been a steady stream of critical publications and adaptations of the works and life of Ghalib set to music, for the stage, TV, and film, which is too long to list here. Today, Ghalib has also percolated deeply into various literatures of the world, including that of the West. The American poet, Adrienne Rich, wrote in her short collection, *Homage to Ghalib*, in 1968:

> How is it Ghalib that your grief, resurrected in pieces,
> Has found its way to this room from your dark house in
> Delhi? (*Leaflets* 68)

Clearly, Ghalib's Persian and Urdu poetry has had a remarkable impact across the world, even as he had a fraught relationship with his contemporary Indo-Persian public sphere. Within the Persian oeuvre, *Temple Lamp* may be argued to be among his finest works. It certainly is among the most popular, both for the importance of its abiding subject (which has acquired renewed importance for its political implications today) as well as its poetic craft. The next section explains the form of the *masnavi*, its poetics, and places it among Ghalib's other masnavis.

2.4 *Temple Lamp*: Poetics

The *masnavi* is a long narrative poem written in *beits* or distiches (a verse in two lines or couplets but making complete sense in themselves) made up of two equal hemistiches or poetic lines called *misra*. Each of these has an internal end-rhyme, so the poem reads with aa, bb, cc . . .

in its rhyme scheme. In *Temple Lamp*, Ghalib has not only given us rhymes but has also followed up with a refrain at the end of each couplet. As an illustration, in the first verse from the poem that follows, the *radif* (refrain) has been represented in bold lettering and the *qafiya* (rhyme) in italics:

nafas bā sūr damsā*zast* **imroz**
khamoshi mahshar-e-rā*zast* **imroz**

The form of the *masnavi* originated in the Middle-Persian period (roughly from the 3rd century BCE to the 9th century CE) and later was adopted in Arabic (where it is also called Muzdawij), Turkish, and Urdu. It has been used mainly for romantic, heroic, and didactic themes, and it became one of the most popular genres of Persianate cultures, including India. Malik Muhammad Jaisi's *Padmavat*, which was adapted into an eponymous film in 2017 and ran into controversies, is a heroic *masnavi* too. The most popular *masnavi* globally is probably the *Masnavi-e-Ma'anavi* or *The Spiritual Masnavi/Verses* by Jalaluddin Balkhi, more popularly known as Rumi. The word '*masnavi*' is derived from the Arabic 'masna' which means 'two by two'. Convention dictates that the metres employed do not exceed eleven syllables in a poetic line. Appropriate metres and diction are also chosen in accordance with the theme of each *masnavi*.

Ghalib has employed the hazaf musaddas mahzuf *bahr* (metre) with the *arkān* (feet) *mafā'ilun mafā'ilun fa'ūlun* in *Chiragh-e-Dair*. It has three *arkān* comprising eleven syllables in total. The first two *arkān* consisting of four syllables each with short-long-long-long vowel rhythm (*mafāʾīlun*) make up the Musaddas. The Mahzuf is the final and shorter *rukn* (foot) with three syllables, with a short-long-long vowel rhythm (*faʾūlun*). The scansion of the first verse of the poem is given below, with the longer syllables in bold, and each foot separated by a slash:

/ na-**fas**-**baa**-**suu** / rᵃ-**dam**-**saa**-zas / tᵃ-**im**-ruz /
/ kha-**mo**-**shii**-mah / sha-**rey**-**raa**-zas / tᵃ-**im**-ruz /[46]

The upbeat and melodious metre, pleasant to the ear, was appropriate for the immense happiness, joy, admiration, and fondness that Ghalib felt for Banaras. It served as the perfect vehicle for his poetic paean to the city.

The scholar Tehseen Firaqi in his essay on *Chiragh-e-Dair* gives us various possible literary sources for the poetic influence on Ghalib for the Banaras poem. *Tūr-e-Maʾrafat* is one such poem by Bedil, whom Ghalib acknowledged in his early career as having had a most powerful impact upon him. Munir Lahori's *Dar Sifat-e Bangālah* and Ghanimat Kunjahi's *Nairang-e-Ishq* are the other poems that make up the literary antecedents.[47] All three poems are by Indo-Persian poets. Shamsur Rehman Faruqi also claims that Ghalib had another Indo-Persian poet, Mulla Sabiq Banarasi's *masnavi, Taʾsir-e-Ishq*, with him as he wrote *Chiragh-e-Dair*.[48]

---

[46] Dr Shad Naved helped me parse this complex *beit*.
[47] Firaqi, 92.
[48] Faruqi, 15.

Temple Lamp is one of Ghalib's eleven Persian masnavis, and the only one dedicated to a city. He wrote no heroic *masnavi*. Narrative poetry does not seem to have been Ghalib's forte. His last *masnavi*, *Abr-i-Guhar-Bār* or *The Cloud that Rains Pearls*, is sometimes argued to be Ghalib's greatest *masnavi*. At 1098 verses, it is much longer than *Chiragh-e-Dair*, and it is written in the Mutaqarib metre. It was meant to be the preamble to a much longer *masnavi* on the holy wars of the prophet that Ghalib never finished. *Abr-i-Guhar-Bar* contains eulogies to Allah, prophet Muhammad and Ali, and books of the minstrel and the cup bearer. It lacks the specific Indianness and the pride of place that *Temple Lamp* evokes for Banaras. It also lacks the autobiographical elements present in *Temple Lamp*.

Besides *Temple Lamp*, Ghalib wrote another *masnavi* on his journey to Calcutta. The aforementioned *Bād-i-Mukhālif* or *The Contrary Wind* is written as a Persian poetics treatise against the critics of Calcutta, in the Khafif metre. It followed upon his criticisms of the Indo-Persian poet, Qatīl, who was popular in Calcutta at the time. The squabble between Ghalib and Qatīl's fans has been mentioned above. The *masnavi* was a supposedly placatory overture from Ghalib, although it continued to criticize Qatīl's style. It remains largely rooted in poetics and has close to nothing about Calcutta, although we know that Ghalib admired the metropolis for its modernity, its cosmopolitanism, and its Persosphere. He wrote Urdu *shers* on it such as this famous one:

kalkatte kā jo zikr kiyā tū ne ham-nashīñ
ík tīr mere sīne meiñ mārā keh hāe hāe

O my friend when you mention Calcutta to me,
You shoot an arrow into my heart; oh!

Surma-e-Binīsh or *The Kohl of the Eyes* in just fifty couplets
written in the Ramal metre is a mystical *masnavi* that
begins with the opening lines of Rumi's *Masnavi-e-Ma'anavi*.
The *Dard-o-Dāgh* or *Pain and Scar* is a didactic poem telling
the life of a peasant in 188 verses in Sari metre. *Rang-o-Bu* or *Colours and Scents* is another narrative and allegorical
poem in 154 verses in the Sari metre. The narrative seeks to
establish the value of the personified *himmat* (magnanimity/
valour) over *daulat* (wealth) and *iqbāl* (fortune). Another
masnavi has the long title *Bayān-e-Numudāri-ye-Shān-e-Nabuwwat-o-vilāyat ki dar-haqiqat partaw-e-nūrul-anwar-e-hazrat-e-ulūhiyat ast* or *The Declaration of the Appearance of the Glory of
Prophecy or Sanctity, which is in Reality the Supreme Light of God*.
It is constituted of 129 verses in Ramal metre and has a
religious, particularly Shia character, venerating Ali. The
remaining four masnavis work as short panegyrics to
different personages, with the longest being forty-two
verses. They are of no great importance. Two of them are
in the metre Sari, one in Hazaj, and one in Ramal.[49]

As evident, *Temple Lamp* is Ghalib's only *masnavi* to be
dedicated to a city, to refer realistically to his material
surroundings, particularly expressing the awe and pleasure

---

[49] More details to be found in Bausani, pp. 392–400.

that he received from Banaras. While metaphysics and religion come in here too, the other poems carry them as their primary themes along with poetics or eulogies and panegyrics to religious-historical or contemporary noble personalities. They are far more abstract and neither engage with the gamut of Indo-Persian philosophies and aesthetics nor with the cultural, environmental, and geopolitical themes in the ways that *Temple Lamp* does.

2.5 *Temple Lamp*: Themes

The final version of *Temple Lamp* that Ghalib circulated and later published contains 108 verses. We know that he wrote other verses on Banaras that he excised from the poem. For example, he sent the following verse along with eleven others in a letter to his friend, Mohammad Ali Khan, but it finds no place in *Temple Lamp*:

> *farangistān-e-husn-e-behijābast*
> *ze khākash zarrā zarrā āftābast*[50]

> This city is the foreign country
> of unveiled beauty,

> Every speck of dust here
> is like the sun.

The number of verses that comprise the text of *Temple Lamp* indicates Ghalib's awareness of Dharmic traditions in which

---

[50] Quoted in Sadiq, p.12.

the figure '108' is regarded as auspicious. In the Shaivite tradition, the Mukhya Shivaganas or chief attendants of Shiva are 108 in number, and hence the *rudrāksha* or the rosary also has 108 beads. In Gaudiya Vaishnavism too, Krishna had 108 *gopīs* or maids in Vrindavan, and hence the mala here too has 108 beads. And while the southern traditions may have not been within Ghalib's purview, there are 108 *divya desams* or temples of Vishnu revered by twelve Alvars, the poet-saints, in the *Divya Prabandha,* the 4,000 verse collections of the Alvars. In Jainism and Buddhism too, the numeral 108 has different significances. Ghalib was clearly paying an obeisance to at least some of these numerological subtleties. The *rudrāksha* would have been definitely within his purview in Banaras as Kashi is the seat of Shiva that he 'never leaves' and therefore also known as Avimukta. Ghalib intended his verses to form a delicately crafted chain of pearls to eulogize Banaras and what it represented to him.

The poem may be divided into different sections according to their themes. Verses 1–5 capture the restlessness of Ghalib's heart. Consider this magnificent verse 3, which pre-empts the teeming yet calming waters of the Ganga to appear in later verses, and expresses the tumult in Ghalib's mind:

> My heart boils in the clamour
> of discontent,
>
> this voiceless bubble
> augurs a storm.

Verses 6–19 convey the pain of being forced to leave his beloved Delhi. They also carry Ghalib's complaints against friends who seem to have forgotten him. This section may be argued to refer to the *Shahr Ashob* tradition of poetry, which is 'the city in tumult' but also 'the lament of the city', the latter often more strongly evident in the Indian poetic tradition. Thus, you have Mir Taqi Mir writing in Urdu in the eighteenth century:

dīdā-e-giryāñ hamāra nahr hai
dil-e-kharāba jaise dilli shahr hai

My weeping eyes are like a stream,
My broken heart like the city of Delhi.

Ghalib decries the apathy of Delhi and his friends in a peevish manner and subsequently claims that he can make a home elsewhere. Verse 11 expresses his sense of loss at having been forced to leave his beloved city as well as his hurt at having been seemingly forgotten by friends:

Not one of my fellow citizens
partakes in my pain,

it is as if I had no country
in the whole world.

A reason for Ghalib to have fled Delhi was also the incessant demands of his creditors. Banaras, poetically, proves to be his romantic and spiritual home. Thus, he moves from loss to reinvigoration, perhaps also recreating in his poetry prophet Muhammad's *hijrat* or migration from Mecca in the face of persecution to Medina—a move that subsequently allowed Islam to flourish and dates the Islamic Hijri calendar. The journey to Calcutta also opened many new vistas for Ghalib, such as his greater investment in Persian poetry and his awareness of technological modernity, and can be considered a major landmark event of his life.

In the next and the longest section, the third, verses 20–81, Ghalib praises Kashi for its natural and transcendental qualities, the beauty of its monuments, its people, and the river Ganga. A most important theme is to describe Banaras as a garden city. This was not just metaphoric symbolism. Until the early nineteenth century, Banaras retained notably green surroundings. This is seen visually in many of James Prinsep's sketches of the city that he made in the 1820s while posted there as a magistrate, probably just a couple of years before Ghalib arrived in Banaras.

Kupuldhara Tulao, Benares

Drawn on Stone by L. Haghe from Sketch by James Prinsep Esqr.

View from Ugneswur Ghat, Benares

Lal Shah's tomb and Ghazimeea ke Durgah Benares

Drawn on stone by George Barnard from a sketch by James Prinsep Esqr. [Originally] printed by C. Hullmandel

Procession of the Tazeeas

During the Mohurrum at the Phatman a Moosulman burying ground, Benares.
Drawn on stone by George Barnard from a sketch by James Prinsep Esqr. [Originally] printed by C. Hullmar

Benares from the Mundakinee tulao

Drawn on stone by J. D. Harding from a sketch by James Prinsep Esqr. [Originally] printed by C. Hullmandel

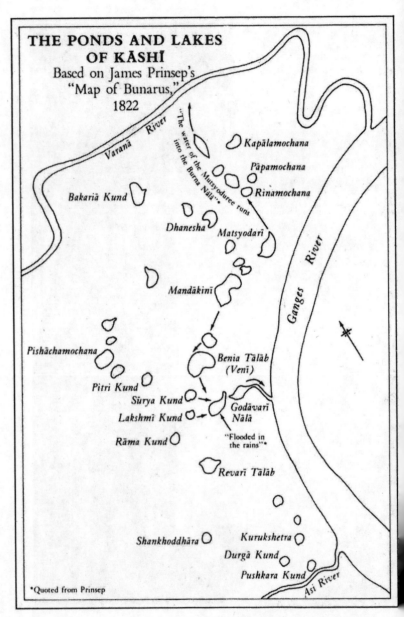

THE PONDS AND LAKES
OF KĀSHĪ
Based on James Prinsep's
"Map of Bunarus,"
1822

Varanā River

"The water of the Matsyoduree runs into the Burna Nālā."

Kapālamochana

Pāpamochana

Rinamochana

Bakariā Kund

Dhanesha

Matsyodari

Ganges River

Mandākinī

Pishāchamochana

Benia Tālāb
(Venī)

Pitri Kund

Sūrya Kund

Godāvari Nālā

Lakshmī Kund

Rāma Kund

"Flooded in the rains"*

Revarī Tālāb

Shankhoddhāra

Kurukshetra

Durgā Kund

Pushkara Kund

Asī River

*Quoted from Prinsep

Quoted from Diana L Eck's *Banaras*

In the map of 'The City of Bunarus' by James Prinsep, published in 1824, one can see that the city is filled with lakes, ponds, and streams.[51] These gradually became polluted and were drained or subsequently dried up in the late-nineteenth century.

Thus, many of the famous markets, streets, or residential areas of modern Banaras are built on these erstwhile waterbodies. Mandakini was one such major lake, which forms the locality of Maidagin today; an important stream was the Godavari, which dried up, and the riverbed is now replaced by the Godaulia Bazaar.

Ghalib's Banaras was this lush green, forested, garden town, with flowing streams and large ponds where—as he tells us in his prose letters, such as the one quoted earlier, and in the third section of the poem—the cool spring breeze blew forever from the east over the Ganga on to the city. It refreshed him and healed him (he says in the letters) after the illness and calumny of Allahabad. Verse 71 establishes this perpetual spring and verdure:

Its forest after forest
is filled with beds of tulips,

its garden after garden
blooms with perpetual spring.

The city as a garden is also evidently a symbol for Eden, paradise, or heaven in the Islamic tradition, as well as the Persian 'pairidaēza'. Fleeing from inhospitable cities, Ghalib

---

[51] Prinsep, p.11; Eck, p.47.

seeks a return to the primordial haven, and the verdant Banaras presents itself as an exuberant paradise. It is in Banaras that he finds his garden of bliss. Thus, in verse 25, he writes:

> May God keep Banaras
> from the evil eye,
>
> it is heavenly bliss,
> paradise established.

In the Persian original of this verse, Ghalib uses the words 'bahisht-e-khurram', 'blissful paradise', which may be compared to 'ānand kānan', a Sanskrit-Hindi name for Banaras that literally means 'pleasure forest'.[52]

The garden of Kashi is also a deeply spiritual place for Ghalib. Thus, in verse 45, he expresses the omnipresence of holiness in this city that makes even thorns flower:

> Each fleck of dirt here
> in its ecstasy is a temple,
>
> every thorn with its verdure
> becomes paradise.

For Ghalib, it is as if Banaras forms a spiritual and physical oasis in a desert, which also resonates with the Arabian *dasht* or desert landscape imagery of the Persianate tradition and

---

[52] Sadiq, p.12.

was ever-present in his Urdu ghazals. Nostalgia for the lost home and the yearning to create or find a new hospitable one may also be traced in these garden images and metaphors. It is here that Ghalib seemed to momentarily lay his finger on the 'garden not yet created' to which he yearned to belong as its 'bulbul' as seen in the Urdu *sher* quoted at the beginning of this essay.

Natural imagery is further employed by Ghalib to create devotional splendour. One can find numerous instances of this in the third section of the poem. To pick but one, a sumptuous image of a holy thread made up of flowers adorned by the breeze is drawn in verse 43 as the wind blows through flower fields:

> Bowing in respect to the very air
> of this garden (that is Banaras),
>
> the spring breeze wears
> a *janéu* made of flowers.[53]

The presence of the deep spirituality and religious devotion in this city is another continuous strain in this section and the following one. Banaras is the place where Hindus come to die to attain salvation. The garden is transformed from the Hebraic paradise into the place for Hindu redemption here as in verse 31:

---

[53] janéu (from Sanskrit): sacred thread that upper-caste Hindu men wear across their chest. The original uses the Persian term *zunnār*.

All captive souls that quit their prisons
from this garden

never again find union
with their bodies.

Banaras is described as the place for ethereal devotion, where people are not concerned with their bodies. The Dharmic quest for release from metempsychosis to find *moksha* is beautifully reiterated in the next verse:

The garden becomes
the wealth of their hopes (of moksha),

The dead (from here) are
eternally alive.

Thus, the spirituality and soulfulness of the city is repeatedly emphasized in *Temple Lamp*. Ghalib privileges Banaras as the most exalted city of Hindustan. Here too, in the title and text of *Temple Lamp*, Ghalib seems to be harking back to Mir Taqi Mir, who wrote in Urdu:

us ke faroġh-e-husn se jhamke hai sab meñ nūr
sham'a-e-haram ho yā ho diyā somnāt kā

Light sparkles everywhere from the aura of His beauty,
Be it the flame of the Kaaba or the lamp of Somnath.

In verse 47 of *Temple Lamp*, probably with an obeisance to Mir, Ghalib draws a parallel between the holiest Muslim site, the Kaaba at Mecca, and the Hindu pilgrimage centre of Kashi:

> The (supreme) place of worship for
> the conch-blowers,
>
> surely, (Banaras) is the Kaaba
> of Hindustan.

For both Mir and Ghalib spirituality transcends organized religion, and they see the same energy at Somnath and Banaras, respectively, as at the Kaaba. This further adds to the import that these poets attach to their eclectic, syncretic spiritual beliefs as they honour Somnath, which is seen today as a site of original Muslim aggression by various Hindutva groups since it was pillaged by Mahmud of Ghazni in 1024 CE. In contrast, one sees a natural ecumenical outlook in Ghalib here and his firm belief in the spiritual capacities of the holiness of Banaras. As Khushwant Singh, author and editor, points out: Ghalib calls Banaras 'Kaa'ba-e-Hindustan (the Mecca of India), not as one would have expected Kaa'ba-e-Hinood (the Mecca of Hindus).'[54] This cosmopolitan and multicultural faith is further confirmed in Ghalib's epistolary correspondences. On 23 December 1859, Ghalib wrote to his friend and disciple Munshi Hargopal Tufta: 'Dearest friend, I consider all humanity to be my family; every man, be he a Muslim or a Hindu or a Christian, is my brother.'[55]

---

[54] Nijhawan p. II.
[55] Quoted in Jafri and Hyder, p. 47.

The following Persian qatā (monothematic verses most commonly four-lines long) by Ghalib asserts (also with a hint of Mir) not just the ecumenical spirituality of Islam and Hinduism but also the cosmopolitanism of his own Persian poetry. It also exhibits its capacity to rival, if not surpass, Persian poetry from Iran on the count of its hybridity in close contact with the Hindu and other non-Islamic cultural traditions of Hindustan:

> *masanj shaukat-e-'urfi keh būd shirāzī*
> *mashū asīr-e-zulālī keh būd khwansārī*
> *ba-somnāt-e-khayālam dar āī tā bīnī*
> *rawan faroz bar dūsh-hāe zunnārī*

> Do not be awed by Urfi even if he is from Shiraz,
> Don't be taken by Zulali though he comes from Khwansar,
> Come into the Somnath of my imagination and see:
> Soul-stirring forms adorned with the *janéu* on my shoulders.

The prowess of Ghalib's poetry thus seems to be enhanced by his spiritual beliefs, Persianate cosmopolitanism, and the composite and syncretic ethos he held as a Hindustani from Delhi who had friends, fans, disciples, and patrons who were Hindu, Christian, and Muslim. Ghalib is emphatic that even if Indo-Persian poetry is written far from Persia, it has its own magnificence. This seems to be derived from its unique contact with non-Islamic culture and philosophy—hence, the Somnath of his imagination, where he welcomes his readers. And in *Temple Lamp*, this multicultural exposure and belief also gives Banaras a greater vibrancy and asserts a cosmopolitan character that one does not find in the same way in mythological sources often looked at by many scholars of the city.

Banaras is the envy of other cities in *Temple Lamp*; the others grudge its glory and pay it their homage. Thus, the metaphor of the circumambulations of a pilgrimage with Banaras being the Kaaba of Hindustan are already built up in verse 22:

> For this (city) has such pride
> of place
>
> that even Delhi comes
> to circle around it.

The idea of Banaras as a cosmopolitan centre that has its place on the global map and on the Silk Route is further established in verses 26 and 70 that call it the envy of China. Verse 86 is where Ghalib collapses spiritual, poetic, and cultural differences between Hindustan and Iran:

> When your madness reaches
> the perfect frenzy,[56]
>
> Kashan[57] from Kashi
> is just a half-step journey.

---

[56] There is a hint of Sufi divine madness that attains perfection and so union with God here.

[57] Kashan: a famous city of Iran, the residents of which were also called Kashi. Ghalib is connecting two major cities of Persia and India here in this verse through a Persianate cosmopolitanism and thus emphasizing a continuity of civilizations.

A continuous thread of intellectual and cultural traditions runs through these faraway cities, which are animated by similar spiritual fervour. Physical distances collapse and Banaras is part of the global ecumene, at par with Kashan, Mecca, and China.

The spiritual glory of Banaras is such that when in verses 72–81 Ghalib asks a dervish why Judgement Day does not arrive on this sinful earth, the clairvoyant responds that God does not wish to destroy Banaras. The spirituality of Banaras is such that in the above-quoted letter to Nawab Muhammad Ali Khan, Ghalib expresses a desire to convert to Hinduism, to absorb the qualities of the city:

> Such an important matter is at hand that if the heart wasn't to be wounded by enemies and foes, I would have given up my religion. I would have broken the rosary and painted a tilak (on my forehead). I would have worn a *janéu* and sat for so long at the banks of the Ganga that all filth would have been washed off me and I would have joined the river like a drop.

This is reflected in the atmosphere Ghalib creates for Banaras in *Temple Lamp*. *Janéu* and tilak are images that get ascribed as symbols to the very elements and all of Banaras is subject to this iconography.

Where spirituality is a major philosophical concern and a strong motif in *Temple Lamp*, Ghalib is also not unaware of the physical beauty he sees around him. One could see this even as an equal engagement, in the Perso-Arabic vein, with the two kinds of love, for the divine and the secular world, *ishq-e-haqīqī* and *ishq-e-majāzī*. This is why the prominent Persian and Urdu scholar and critic Tahseen Firaqi argues that Ghalib has created a luminous and moving picture through the three sensitivities of touch, sight, and hearing in *Chiragh-e-Dair*.[58] We have already discussed the euphonic metre and rhythm of the poem above. The visual and tactile is seen and felt in Ghalib's various descriptions, most strongly in this third section.

The natural beauty of Banaras as a garden city has also been discussed above. Ganga is also a powerful, teeming river that rubs its forehead at the feet of Banaras to be hailed holy. It is what grants Banaras its final touches of beauty, as in verse 64:

> Or one could behold Banaras,
> perhaps, as the beauty
>
> who preens from dawn to dusk
> with the Ganga as a mirror in their hand.

The river is of course central to the ritual and cultural sense of the town today, just as it has been for millennia. But Ghalib also reminds us of a pristine ecology, when the river flowed unhindered and was crystal clear for the city to behold its reflection in. We must remember that the term for 'settlement', 'population', and even 'life' in Persian (and Urdu-Hindi) is *'aabādī'* with *'aab'* or water as its root word. The Ganga and Banaras are complementary.

---

[58] Firaqi, p.73.

View of the Ganges

From the phatak or gate at the top of Punchgunga ghat.
Drawn on stone by William Walten from a sketch by James Prinsep Esqr. [Originally] printed by C. Hullmar

And it is when they are bathing in the river that Ghalib admires the beauties of Banaras. They are described with the greatest delicacy, but their bodies communicate the greatest zest for life, giving shape to the water (verse 60), making the poet-narrator fall for them. A particularly sensuous yet elegant image is given in verse 57, when the narrator suggests that the gentle manner of the bathing of devotees grants honour to the river itself, rather than the other way round:

> Their gestures of bathing
> grant
>
> each wave
> the good tidings of honour.

We know that Ghalib admitted in an undated letter, probably from around 1860, that he had fallen for a *domni* or a courtesan about forty years earlier.[59] It is commonly believed that this was a singer called Nawab Jan, whom he met around the time of his wedding to Umrao Begum. One wonders, and this is only academic conjecture, if perhaps it could have been (also?) in Banaras that he had lost his heart? The Aurangabad area Ghalib was staying in was not far from the residences of the famous *tawaifs* or courtesans of the time at Dalmandi. Ghalib did extend his stay longer than he had planned, without meeting anyone of consequence. We do not know precisely what transpired,

---

[59] See Russell and Islam, p.42.

but *Temple Lamp* is rich with sensuous descriptions of the beautiful physicality of the people of Banaras. Others such as the early Ghalib critic, Malik Ram, have also argued for the possibility of a paramour or object of admiration. Ram cited Ghalib's following Persian verse (not included in *Temple Lamp*) as evidence:

> *kāsh kāñ but-e-kāshī dar pazer dam Ghālib*
> *bandah tawām goyam, gavīdam, zanāz, ārī.* [60]

I wish that idol of Banaras would accept Ghalib,
I would say I am your slave, and they'd respond proudly,
yes!

Thus, *Temple Lamp*, which is more autobiographical or descriptive of event and place than the far more abstract ghazals, illustrates Ghalib's penchant for physical beauty, his ability to perceive and represent pleasure and joy, and his zest for life. This contradicts descriptions of Ghalib as primarily a poet of grief. Ali Sardar Jafri, the famous Urdu poet, tells that Ghalib mixes joy with grief: [it is] 'impossible to separate the concord of joy and sorrow in Ghalib's poems . . . [it would be] wrong to call him the poet of melancholy or the singer of joy. Ghalib sings of the joyous splendour of agony.'[61]

The next two sections of the *masnavi* show us this merging of joy, grief, and even doubt very well. Section

---

[60] Firaqi, p.75.
[61] Jafri and Hyder, p.10

four (verses 82–102) laments Ghalib's misfortune and describes a sense of guilt at having abandoned his family in Delhi, while he has prospered in Banaras and relished its spiritual and material comforts. He feels the need to break through the bonds of the city. In verse 85, he even speaks of creating his personal heaven out of his grief. Section five or the final six beits (verses 103–108) speak in a Sufi manner of *fanā* or annihilation of the self to care for others or be one with God, and of 'extinguishing the rest' (108).

Much later in life, Ghalib wrote to a friend, Miyandad Khan Saiyyid, in a letter: 'Banaras is beyond words. Such cities are seldom created. I happened to be there at the height of my youth. If I were young now, I would go and live there and not return.'[62]

Let us now tour Banaras through the craft of Ghalib's pen.

2.6 Works Cited

Asif, Manan Ahmed. *The Loss of Hindustan: The Invention of India*. Cambridge: Harvard University Press, 2020.

Bausani, A. 'Ghalib's Persian Poetry.' *Ghalib: Life, Letters and Ghazals*. pp. 390–413. New Delhi: Oxford University Press, 2007.

Begum, Sagheer-un-Nisa. *Ghazaliyat-e-Ghalib ka Aroozi Tajziya*. New Delhi: Maktaba Jamia, 1984. Urdu.

Bilal, Maaz Bin. Trans. 'Children's Play.' from Urdu of ghazal '*bazicha-e-atfāl*'. Mirza Ghalib. *Indiana Review*.

---

[62] Farooqi, p.96.

Winter 2017, Vol. 39 Number 2. 94–95. ISSN: 0738-386X. Print.

Ciotti, Manuela. 'Ethnohistories behind local and global bazaars: Chronicle of a Chamar weaving community in the Banaras region.' *Contributions to Indian Sociology* (n.s.) 41, 3 (2007): 321–54.

Desai, Madhuri. 'Mosques, Temples, and Orientalists: Hegemonic Imaginations in Banaras.' *Traditional Dwellings and Settlements Review*, Fall 2003, Vol. 15, No. 1, pp. 23–37.

Eaton, Richard M. 'Temple Desecration and Indo-Muslim States.' *Frontline*. 5 January 2001.

---. 'The Persian Cosmopolis (900–1900) and the Sanskrit Cosmopolis (400–1400).' *The Persianate World: Rethinking a Shared Sphere*. Ed. Abbas Amanat, and Assef Ashraf. Leiden: Brill, 2015.

Eck, Diana L. *Banaras: City of Light*. 1983. New Delhi: Penguin, 2015.

Farooqi, Mehr Afshan. *Ghalib: A Wilderness at My Doorstep*. New Delhi: Penguin, 2020.

Faruqi, Shamsur Rahman. *Ghalib Par Char Tehreerein*. New Delhi: Ghalib Institute, 2001. Print.

Firaqi, Tahseen. *Ghalib: Fikr-o-Aahang*. New Delhi: Ghalib Institute, 2012. Urdu.

Ghalib, Mirza. *Dīwān-e-Ghālib Dehlavi*. Ed. Doctor Syed Taqi Abedi. Teheran: Intishārat-e-Baaz, 2010. Persian.

---. *Kulliyat-e-Ghalib*. Lucknow: mutabbe' Munshi Nawal Kishore, 1925. Persian

---. *Kulliyat-e-Ghalib: Farsi*. 3 vols. Ed. Doctor Syed Taqi Abedi. New Delhi: Ghalib Insitute, Delhi. Persian.

---. *Kulliyat-e-Ghalib: Farsi*. 3 vols. Ed. Sayyad Murtaza Hussain Fazil Lakhnawi. Lahore: Majlis Taraqqi-e-Adab, 1967. Persian.

---. *Kulliyat-e-Ghalib: Mukammil Kalam-e-Farsi, Mirza Asadullah Khañ Ghalib*. Ed. Amir Hasan Noorani. Lucknow: (Raja) Ram Kumar Book, waris mutabbe' Munshi Nawal Kishore, 1968. Persian.

Hali, Altaf Husain. *Yadgar-e-Ghalib*. 1897. Delhi: Maktaba Jamia, 2015. Urdu.

Jafri, Ali Sardar, and Qurratulain Hyder. *Ghalib: His Life and Poetry*. New Delhi: Stirling, 2002.

Kinra, Rajeev. 'Fresh Words for a Fresh World: *Taza-Gu'i* and the Poetics of Newness in Early Modern Indo-Persian Poetry.' *Sikh Formations*. Vol. 3, No. 2, December 2007, pp. 125–149.

Kumar, Nita. 'The Mazars of Banaras: a New Perspective on the City's Sacred Geography.' *National Geographical Journal of India*, Vol. 33, No. 3 (1987), pp. 263–267.

Mahuli, Shahid. *Ghalib aur Banaras*. New Delhi: Ghalib Institute, 2010. Urdu.

Meisami, Julie Scott. 'Allegorical Gardens in the Persian Poetic Tradition: Nezami, Rumi, and Hafez.' *International Journal of Middle Eastern Studies*. Vol. 17 (1985), pp. 229-260.

Nijhawan, P. K. *Kaa'ba-e-Hindustan: Chirag-e-Dair*. Mumbai: English Edition Publishers & Distributors (India), 2005. Persian, Urdu, Hindi, English.

Naim, C. M. 'Ghalib's Delhi: A Shamelessly Revisionist Look at Two Popular Metaphors.' *Annual of Urdu Studies*, Vol. 18 (2003).

Narang, Gopichand. *Ghalib: Innovative Meanings and the Ingenious Mind*. Trans. Surinder Deol. New Delhi: OUP, 2017.

Noorani, Yaseen. 'The Lost Garden of al-Andalus: Islamic Spain and the Poetic Inversion of Colonialism.' *International Journal of Middle East Studies*, Vol. 31, No. 2 (May 1999), pp. 237–254.

Prigarina, Natalia. *Mirza Ghalib: A Creative Biography*. Tr. from Russian by M. Osama Faruqi. Karachi: OUP, 2000.

Princep, James. *Benares Illustrated: in a Series of Drawings*. 1833. Varanasi: Vshwavidyalaya Prakashan, 1996.

Rich, Adrienne. *Leaflets: Poems from 1965–1968*. New York: Norton, 1969.

Russell, Ralph and Islam. *Ghalib: Life and Letters*. 1969. New Delhi: OUP, 2000.

Rekhta.org.

Sadiq. Trans. and Introduced. *Chiragh-e-Dair: Banaras par Kendrit Kavitaen*. Mirza Ghalib. New Delhi: Rajkamal, 2018. Hindi.

Sadiq. Ed. *Masnavi Chiragh-e-Dair: Ma'a Paanch Urdu Taraajim*. Delhi: Urdu Academy, 2015. Urdu.

Sharma, Sunil. 'The City of Beauties in Indo-Persian Poetic Landscape.' *Comparative Studies of South Asia, Africa and the Middle-East*. Vol. 24, No. 2, 2004.

Silver, Brian Quayle. *The Noble Science of the Ghazal: The Urdu Poetry of Mirza Ghalib*. New Delhi: Manohar, 2015.

Singh, Rana P. B. 'On Banaras: Ghalib's *The Lamp of the Temple*.' *Cultural Landscapes and the Lifeworld: Literary Images of Banaras (Kashi)*. pp. 128–138. Varanasi: Indica Books, 2004.

Verma, Pavan K. *Ghalib: The Man, The Times*. 1989. New Delhi: Penguin, 2008.

Williams, Philippa. *Everyday Peace?: Politics, Citizenship and Muslim Lives in India*. Chichester: Wiley Blackwell, 2015.

Yarshater, E. 'Some Common Characteristics of Persian Poetry and Art.' *Studia Islamica*. Vol. 16, 1962, pp. 61-71.

'Yawar', Yaqoob Ali Khan. 'Ghalib, Banaras, aur Masnavi *Chiragh-e-Dair*'. *Ghalib aur Banaras*. Ed. Shahid Mahuli. pp. 152–176. New Delhi: Ghalib Institute, 2010. Urdu.

Zaidi, Ali Jawad. *A History of Urdu Literature*. 1993. New Delhi: Sahitya Akademi, 2017.

Zoe, Ansari. *Masnaviyaat-e-Ghalib: Asl Fārsi ma'a Urdu Taraajim*. New Delhi: Ghalib Insititute, 1983. Persian and Urdu.

Note on the Translation
and on Collating the Original
Persian Text

In keeping with Walter Benjamin's suggestions regarding the task of the translator, when I translate a poem, it is important for me to translate not just its meaning but also its rhythms and formal concerns, such that the translation has a form of its own, somewhat akin to the original. A *masnavi* is a long poem usually written in end-rhyming distiches. Mirza Ghalib's *masnavi*, *Chiragh-e-Dair*, has further added refrains following the end-rhymes. I sought to recreate the prosody of this original while transmitting its meaning accurately in an appropriate form that would be consistent throughout in doing justice to the form of the distich itself and the *masnavi* as a whole. While it did not seem possible to translate the compounded Persian verses into distiches in English with a consistent metre or rhyme, I felt that maintaining the essential feature of the *beit* (*sher* in Urdu) or distich—the even division of the verse with its exposition in the first line and the resolution or response in the second—had to be maintained at any cost. It allows each *beit* its great balance in the original and had to be recreated in the target language one way or the other. There is a *rabt*, a bond or link which works like a spark or charge of contact that flows across the first *misra*, the poetic line or the hemistich, which is the exposition, to the second *misra*, which provides the resolution. Hence, I have translated each *beit* or couplet most often into two couplets. In a few instances, I have managed to translate a Persian couplet into an English couplet. This even division of each verse in the translation as in the original allows the original *rabt* to be transmitted to the translation as well. I have not tried to retain rhymes or refrain or metre like the original as it did not seem possible to retain them throughout, and to do so in an uneven manner would have proved more harmful or jarring than faithful.

In a few places, I have inserted parenthetical phrases that bring in information, interpretation, or insight that may have been more easily accessible to readers of the Persian or Urdu tradition but may leave some difficulties or confusions for the anglophone readers. Sometimes, the parentheses also carry words or phrases that the English translation forces me to include for grammatical and/or stylistic reasons, even though the original Persian worked well without their equivalents. I expect the reader of my translation to read the parenthetical phrases in continuity with the main text, as part of the verse and its rhythm, but with the knowledge that while this information was implied in the original, it is made explicit here by the translator. In fewer places, I have used footnotes to give entirely allusive and not immediately employed information.

I have also used the plural pronoun 'they' and its accusative and possessive cases 'them' and 'their' to refer to the epicene or gender-neutral singular pronoun from Persian. While the implication in these lines is often to a particular woman or perhaps a group of women, one cannot be sure. The original Persian (and also Urdu) poetry allows for fascinating gender ambiguities that would have been entirely lost had I used 'she' or 'her' instead.

I had thought of using the Persian and Urdu 'Dehlī' for the capital city 'Delhi' in the English translation first but dropped it later upon careful consideration arising from some strong suggestions. It does remain important for different readers to recognize Delhi's different names, especially its Persian cognate Dehlī, apart from its anglicized Delhi, but it seemed to jar too much with English readers. To expect even Ghalib to change the standard anglicized form of the city name for its non-native people in 2022 is perhaps too much to ask.

Another interesting lexical choice for me was translating the Persian word '*zunnar*' to the Sanskrit-Hindi-Urdu '*janéu*' rather than the English 'sacred thread'. A sacred thread can be worn on the wrist, the neck, the arm or even the ankle. A *zunnar* or janéu is specifically the sacred thread worn by Brahmin or other upper-caste men diagonally across their chest. 'Sacred thread' would have meant using two words in place of one, and would have been less precise. For an international audience I could keep even *zunnar* as is, and in certain verses it even flows better, but *janéu* seemed most accessible to Indian audiences, although translating from Persian into English but bringing in a Sanskrit word does feel risky.

I was encouraged most strongly to undertake this translation by Prof. Sadiq (former Head, Department of Urdu, University of Delhi), who has himself completed a Hindi translation of *Chiragh-e-Dair*. He has also edited an Urdu edition of the Banaras poem where he has collated multiple Urdu translations of each of the 108 verses. The translators whose work is included here are: Zoe Ansari, Akhtar Hasan, Sardar Jafri, Hanif Naqvi, and Kalidas Gupta Reza. My translation has benefitted greatly from the work of all of these translators of the Persian into Hindi and Urdu, and I remain indebted to Sadiq Sahab for his labours in bringing this work to my attention and pushing me to undertake this project.

My translation process involved reading the Persian original and all the six Hindi-Urdu translations originally at my disposal, often chasing up words and etymologies across languages and then writing my English versions of the verses. I also looked at the partial English translations of *Chiragh-e-Dair* by Natalia Prigarina, Qurattulain Hyder and Ali Sardar Jafri, Mehr Afshan Faruqi, and Rana P. B. Singh, although my English translation practice is quite independent of theirs. Having completed the translation, the Hindi and English translations by P. K. Nijhawan were brought to my notice by Prof. Frances Pritchett. It was too late for these translations to really impact my own, although I could see that Nijhawan's couplets were quite different from my own pairs of couplets for each original. He has retained end-rhymes, courting the risk of sometimes introducing unnatural English verse and straying far from meaning at times too.

My English-language poet friends who read my translation and gave extensive comments also contributed to the quality of the work. Uttaran Das Gupta is often my first reader, and he commented on multiple drafts. Dr Arun Sagar made detailed suggestions that led to structural changes and new line breaks in my translation. My deepest thanks to both. Friend and colleague Dr Irfanullah Farooqi gave invaluable suggestions to improve the introduction as did my dear PhD supervisor, Dr Daniel Roberts, whose devotion to my work has never dimmed; my gratitude to them. Prof. Anisur Rahman also gave encouraging comments on the work. My colleague and friend Ms Bilquees Daud read over the Persian translation diligently and also made some suggestions on the translation. This is a better book for her intervention. My dear friend, senior colleague, and, dare I say, mentor Dr Shad Naved provided most astute feedback on various nitty-gritties of Persian and particularly helped me understand the Persian metre much better.

Working on *Chiragh-e-Dair* over an extensive period of time I discovered that the original text across its different editions had numerous errors and mistakes, which I was not fully equipped to correct on my own. I sought out different Persian scholars to help me prepare an authoritative text that I could work with for my translation. My old college friend Dr Naved Jafri accompanied me to the two Ghalib institutes of Delhi, as well as the Iran Culture House and the Anjuman-Taraqqi-e-Urdu, to hunt down even more editions of Ghalib's Persian poetry. Dr. Mufti Mushtaq Ahmed Tijarwi, author of *Ghalib aur Alwar*, read with me parts of the original poem from a number of different editions, helping me correct mistakes such as '*ālā bayāney*' (verse 4) to '*lā bayāney*'. He also narrated many anecdotes of Ghalib and pointed me to different sources.

The renowned Persian authority, Prof. Akhlaque Ahmad Ansari 'Ahan', of JNU helped me confirm and correct other misprints such as '*bailāq*' to '*yailāq*' (verse 41). Mistakes such as where '*dāgh-e-chashm*' (verse 33) (literally wound/scar of the eye) has been wrongly printed as '*dāgh-e-jism*' (wound/scar of the body) in many editions has led to different (and wrong?) Urdu translations. Hanif Naqvi, for example, has translated this as 'wound/scar of the body' in his Urdu translation. Ghalib was well aware of the multiple valences and the difficulty of meaning of his verse and proudly declared in the Urdu *sher*:

ganjīna-e-ma'anī kā tilism us ko samajhiye
jo lafz keh ghālib mere ash'ār meñ aave

Think it the magic of the treasure trove of meaning,
That word, Ghalib, which features in my verse.

The possibilities of meaning in Ghalib are always such, and the difficulty and complexity in interpretation so great that readers and translators strive to find meaning even in misprints and other such errors.

Prof. Ahan also helped clarify certain doubts about reading different verses. Even more generously, he sat with me for hours to recite the original, which allowed me to transcribe it correctly into the *Sabk-e-Hindi* accent in Roman script in this book. The original Persian does not explicitly use diacritics, and there are often variances between individuals as well as Iranians and South-Asians in their accents. I wished to stick to the Indo-Persian accent as that would have been closest to Ghalib's own way of speaking, perhaps. It also made sense to transcribe this Indo-Persian poem with the Indo-Persian accent of today rather than the Persian where they do not have the Indo-Persian nasal 'ñ' nor end lines with '-ey' as they end them with 'ī' such as in *'bayāney'*, which in the Iranian accent would be written as *'bayānī'*. My most sincere thanks to 'Ahan' sahab for his immense generosity.

The scholar Dr Prashant Keshavmurthy had peer reviewed the book, and a lot of the concerns regarding the text, my transliteration, and certain conceptions in the Introduction were first highlighted by him. He also suggested alternative translations to different verse, some of which I accepted. This work has benefitted immensely from his inputs, even as I have not accepted all his suggestions and the errors that remain are mine. Dr Pasha Khan had also provided some suggestions about transcriptions etc.

To all of these Persian savants, I am forever indebted.

My new colleague and friend Dr Mohammed Sayeed was available often to read over the original and my translation together, and we discussed many minute details regarding translational choices and conceptual questions and even design ideas. Dr Lipika Kamra, colleague and dear friend, diligently read over multiple drafts and gave the best feedback I needed as it came from a new Ghalib reader. My mother is my first go-to resource for my daily struggles with Urdu and Persian vocabulary and poetic meanings. She is the perfect sounding board without whom I may not have ever worked on Urdu or Persian. For her, always, my love and respect.

Upon the conclusion of the book, many scholars, poets, translators—senior colleagues, friends and acquaintances—saw some value in the work and responded kindly to requests for blurbs. To them, in alphabetic order, my profuse thanks and gratitude: Mr. Ashok Vajpeyi, Prof. Frances Pritchett, Gulzar, Prof. Mehr Afshan Farooqi, Dr. Prashant Keshvamurthy and Mr. Ranjit Hoskote. And to the Raza Foundation I remain ever grateful for allowing me to use Sayed Haider Raza's exquisitely beautiful and perfectly apt painting of Banaras for the cover of this book.

Finally, a warm thanks to my friend and agent Kanishka Gupta for finding a suitable home in English for Ghalib and me, and to the editors and designers at Penguin Random House India for their work on this volume.

TEMPLE
LAMP

1.

nafas bā sūr damsāzast imroz
khamoshi mahshar-e-rāzast imroz

Today, my breath conjoins the notes of the *Sūr* (of Isrāfil),[1]
and my silence tends to become the plains of Hashr;[2]

today,
all secrets will be unveiled.

---

[1] Sūr: Trumpet of doom. Isrāfil the archangel (counterpart of the Biblical Raphael) will blow this trumpet from a holy rock in Jerusalem before Armageddon, leading to the day of the resurrection of souls.

[2] The plains of Hashr are where all souls will be judged on their good and evil acts, and all veils unveiled.

2.

rag-e-sangam, sharāre-mī-nawīsam
kaf-e-khākam, ghubāre-mī-nawīsam

I am the vein of stone,
my writing sparks.

I am a fistful of dirt,
I write dust storms (of the heart).

3.

dil az shor-e-shikayathā bajosh ast
habāb-e-be-nawā tūfañ kharosh ast

My heart boils in the clamour
of discontent,

this voiceless bubble
augurs a storm.

4.

balab dāram zamīre lā bayāney
nafas khuñ-kun jigar pālā fughāney

My conscience seeks
to break its silence through my lips,

my heart is strained to turn
my breath bloody in complaint.

5.

pareshāñ-tar ze-zulfam dāstānīst
be-da'vā har sar-e-mūyam zabanīst

My tale is more tangled
than (my beloved's) long hair,

each strand on my body
is a tongue risen in complaint.

6.

shíkāyat gona-e-dāram ze-ahbāb
katān-e-khesh mī shoyam ba-mahtāb

I complain to my friends
as if—

the *katāñ* cloth[3] will be washed
in moonlight only to be ripped.

---

[3] The katāñ cloth is supposed to be so delicate that it is shredded by moonlight.

7.

dar ātish az nawā-e-sāz-e-khesham
kabābe-shu'la-e āwāz-e-khesham

I burn in the lament
of my own lute,

a kebab on the flame
of my own song.

8.

nafas abreshame sāz-e-fughānast
basāne nai tabam dar ustkhwānast

On the harp of lament,
my each breath forms a chord,

like a flute,
my bones are filled with fire.

9.

muhīt afgandah bairūñ gauharam rā
chū gard afshāñdah āhan jauharam rā

The way the sea spews pearls,
(I too have left Delhi),[4]

how iron expels its jewels,
thinking them cheap dust.

---

[4] The Persian, Urdu original city name is dehlī, which became Delhi in English.

10.

ze dehlī tā buruñ āwurdah bakhtam
ba tūfān-e-taghāful dādah rakhtam

From the moment destiny
threw me out of Delhi,

I was thrown into tumultuous storms,
expelled from memory.

•

11.

kas az ahl-e-watan ghamkhār-e-man nīst
marā dar dahr pindāre watan nīst

Not one of my fellow citizens
partakes in my pain,

it is as if I had no country
in the whole world.[5]

---

[5] Watan: a unit of spatial belonging that often signified nothing larger
than a city, so a 'country' for such individuals as Ghalib could be limited
to their city, which was Delhi in the poet's case. Alternatively, it could be
a country within a country, in that sense implying different and multiple
loci of belonging, so Ghalib could think of himself belonging to Delhi,
Hindustan, and the larger Persianate cosmopolitan world.

12.

za arbāb-e-watan joyam seh tan rā
ke rang-o-raunaq and īñ nuh chaman rā

I seek three from among
the lords of my country,

who are the light and lustre
of these nine gardens.[6]

---

6 Nine gardens: after the convention of nine skies, used here to refer to
 Ghalib's Delhi, a city made up of nine (historical) cities.

13.

chū khud rā jalwā sanj-e-nāz khāham
ham az haq fazl-e-haq rā bāz khāham

When my heart wishes
to feel proud (of my friends),

I seek by God's grace
to meet Fazl-e-Haq.[7]

---

[7] Fazl-e-Haq Khairabadi (1796–1861): A nineteenth-century Hanafi jurist, philosopher (in the Aristotelian-Islamic Peripatetic tradition whose contributions included a novel theory of time in response to Newtonian physics), scholar, and poet who was sentenced to *kālā pānī* (sent to Cellular Jail in the Andaman Islands) during the mutiny retributions post-1857. He was a dear friend of Ghalib, possibly because of Ghalib's deep investment in philosophy as reflected in Ghalib's poetry as well. 'Fazl-e-Haq' also means 'the grace of truth/justice' or 'the grace of God' and Ghalib employs wordplay in the original verse. Khairabadi's line has since produced great poets and film personalities (lyricist, actors, directors): Muztar Khairabadi (grandson), Jan Nisar Akhtar (great grandson), Javed Akhtar and Salman Akhtar (sons of Jan Nisar), Farhan Akhtar and Zoya Akhtar (children of Javed), and Kabir Akhtar (son of Salman). His book on philosophy, *Hadiyatul-Saeediya*, is taught widely in madrassahs in India and as far as Egypt.

14.

chū hirz-e-bāzū-e-īmāñ nawīsam
Hisāmuddin Haider Khāñ nawīsam

When I inscribe an amulet
for the arm of my faith,

'Hisāmuddin Haider Khāñ',[8]
I write upon it.

---

[8] A much older, but close friend and champion of Mirza Ghalib; originally
a friend of his father in law. Hisamuddin Haider Khan was a poet and
the student of Mir Taqi Mir and Mir Khalīq. He died in 1846. A haveli
in his name still stands in Old Delhi's Ballimaran locality.

15.

chū paiwand-e-qabā-ey jāñ tarāzam
Amīnuddīn Ahmed Khāñ tarāzam

When I wish to darn a patch
on the cloak of my soul,

the sole label I remember
is 'Aminuddin Ahmed Khan'.[9]

---

[9] Ghalib's dear friend and a cousin of his wife, he was the second Nawab of Loharu, the eldest son of Nawab Ahmed Bakhsh Khan.

16.

giraftam kaz jahānābād raftam
mar-īnāñ rā chirā az yād raftam

I admit I have come away
from the city of Delhi,

but how have my friends
forgotten me so quickly?

17.

mago dāgh-e-firāq-e-bostāñ sokht
gham-e-be-mehrī-e-īñ dostāñ sokht

It is not the wound of separation
from the garden (of Delhi) that burns,

what burns is
the inconsideration of my friends.

18.

jahānābād gar nabuwad alam nīst
jahānābād bādā jāe kam nīst

Even if I have lost Delhi,[10]
why must I grieve?

may the world prosper,
there is no dearth of cities.

---

[10] Ghalib uses the diminutive form, *Jahānābād*, of the name Shahjahanabad of his Delhi. While Shahjahanabad means "founded by (the Mughal emperor) Shahjahan", Jahanabad can imply 1. 'Shahjahanabad', 2. "founded by Jahān or the world," and finally 3. "may the world prosper." Ghalib is building on these puns over the distich.

19.

nabāshad qahat bahr-e-āshyāne
sar-e-shākh-e-gule dar gulsitāne

There is no dearth of space
to make a nest,

I will find a flowering bough
in a garden.

20.

sipas dar lālah zāre jā tawāñ kard
watan rā dāgh-e-istighna tawāñ kard

One can, thus, make place
in a garden of Tulips.

and turn the home-city
into the mark of renunciation.[11]

---

[11] *Istighna* is a preliminary stage of Sufism, implying material renunciation.

21.

bakhātir dāram ainak gul zamīne
bahār āīñ sawād-e-dil nashīne

I welcome now
a flowering land,

spring settles here
on the horizon of the heart.

22.

keh mī āyad be-da'wa gāh-e-lāfash
jahānābad az bahr-e-tawāfash

For this (city) has such pride
of place

that even Delhi comes
to circle around it.[12]

---

[12] Reminiscent of Haj where pilgrims circumambulate the Kaaba.

23.

nigah rā dā'va-e-gulshan adāī
azāñ khurram bahār-e-āshnāī

The eye boasts garden graces[13]
(having seen Banaras),

whence the joy
of the springtime of intimacy.

---

[13] Banaras is both an external source for the poet's imaginative writing, but also created and embellished through his eye and pen. The outward spectacle is rooted in the poet's eye, and one gives power and value to the other.

24.

sukhan rā nāzish-e-mīnū qamāshī
zi gulbāng-e-satāish.hāe kāshi

Poetry attains its pride (of place)
in heaven

when it
sings paeans in praise of Kashi.

25.

ta'ālallah banāras chashm-e-bad dūr
bahisht-e-khurram-o-firdaus-e-ma'mūr

May God keep Banaras
from the evil eye,

it is heavenly bliss,
paradise established.

26.

banāras rā kase guftā ke chīn ast
hanūz az gang chīnash bar jabīn ast

Someone once compared the beauty
of Banaras to China,

and since that day its brow is wrinkled
with the bend of the Ganga.

27.

bakhush purkāri-e-tarz-e-wajūdash
ze dehlī mī rasad har dam darūdash

Delighted with its modes,
the ways of being (of Banaras),

with each breath,
Delhi sends its blessings (for Kashi).[14]

---

[14] Blessings: *darūd* is an Islamic prayer usually in praise of Muhammad, in this case applied for praises for Kashi.

28.

banāras rā magar dīdast dar khāb
ke mī gardad ze nehrash dar dahan āb

Were the eyes of (Delhi's) dreams
transfixed at Banaras?

is that why its mouth drools now
with the waters of its canal?[15]

---

[15] Ghalib's Delhi or Shahjehanabad was watered by the Sa'adat Khan canal
which flowed in Chandni Chowk till 1910, when it was paved over by the
British. This canal had watered the lush gardens on the northern side of
Chandni Chowk.

29.

hasūdash guftan āīn-e-adab nīst
wa lekin ghibtah gar bāshad ajab nīst

To call it the envy (of Delhi)
would be discourtesy,

but it should be no wonder
that there is jealousy.

30.

tanāsukh mashrabāñ chūñ lab goshāyand
be-kesh-e-khesh kāshī rāstāyand

When they open their lips,
the believers in reincarnation,

they sing praises of Kashi,
they have their reasons.

31.

ke harkas kāndarāñ gulshan bimīrad
digar paiwand-e-jismān-e-nagīrad

All captive souls that quit their prisons
from this garden

never again find union
with their bodies.

32.

chaman sarmāya-e-ummīd gardad
ba-murdan zindā-e-jāvīd gardad

The garden becomes
the wealth of their hopes (of moksha),

The dead (from here) are
eternally alive.

33.

zahe āsūdgī bakhsh-e-rawānhā
ke dāgh-e-chashm mī shūyad ze jānhā

All praise to this city
that grants contentment to souls,

it removes the evil eye,
makes whole.

34.

shagufte nīst az āb-o-hawāyash
ke tanhā jāñ shawad andar fazāyash

It is no wonder
that from its climate,

in its ambience,
one should become pure soul.

35.

bayā ai ghāfil az kaifīyat-e-nāz
nigāhe bar parīzādānash andāz

Those of you unacquainted
with pride,

come here, cast an eye
on its fairy-born ones.

36.

hamah jānhāe be-tan kun tamāshā
nadārad āb-o-khāk īñ jalwah hāshā

Behold: the tamasha
of these souls without bodies,

their spectacle bears no concern
with water or dust.

37.

nihād-e-shāñ chu bū-e-gul girāñ nīst
hamah jānand jisme darmiyāñ nīst

Their being is light,
like the fragrance of roses,

they are pure life and soul,
the body does not intervene.

38.

khas-o-khārash gulistān ast goī
ghubārash jauhar-e-jān ast goī

Even straw and thorn
become the garden (of paradise) here,
as it were,

its dust turns into the jewel
of the soul,
as it were.

39.

darīñ dairīnā dairistān-e-nairang
bahārash aimanast az gardish-e-rañg

In this ancient temple-
city of magic,

its spring is free
from change of colour.

40.

cheh farwardīñ cheh deī māh-o-cheh murdād
bahar mausam fazāyash jannat ābād

Be it in spring, or in summer, or winter,
the weather here each season is that of heaven.

41.

bahārāñ dar shitā-o-saif ze āfāq
bekāshī mī kunad qishlāq-o-yailāq

Escaping the bleakest winters
and scorching summers,

spring pitches winter
and summer camps in Kashi.

42.

buwad dar 'arz-e-bāl afshānī-e-nāz
khazānash sandal-e-peshānī-e-nāz

Autumn, when it shakes its wings
in pride,

becomes on (Kashi's) forehead
a proud sandalwood mark.[16]

---

[16] Tilak: The ceremonial markings a number of Hindus of sects make on their foreheads using sandalwood paste often after a puja (prayer).

43.

bah-taslīm-e-hawā-e-āñ-chaman-zār
zemauj-e-gul-bahārāñ bastah zunnār

Bowing in respect to the very air
of this garden (that is Banaras),

the spring breeze wears
a *janéu* made of flowers.[17]

---

[17] Janéu (Sanskrit, Hindi-Urdu) or zunnar (Persian, Hindi-Urdu): Sacred thread worn across the chest by Hindu upper-caste men since their coming-of-age thread ceremony, as a sign of their great piety. Brahmins are thought of as being twice born due to this ritual.

44.

falak rā qashqah ash gar bar jabīñ nīst
pas īñ rangīnī-e-mauj-e-shafaq chīst

If it not be a *tílak*
on the forehead of the sky,

then pray, tell, what is
that many-hued wave of twilight?

45.

kaf-e-har-khākash az mastī kanishtey
sar-e-har khārash az sabzī bahishtey

Each fleck of dirt here
in its ecstasy is a temple,

every thorn with its verdure
becomes paradise.

46.

sawādash pāe-takht-e-butparastāñ
sarāpāyash zíyāratgāh-e-mastāñ

This settlement is the seat
of the idol-worshipping faithful,

from beginning to end
it is the pilgrimage of mystics.

47.

ibādatkhāna-e-nāqūsiyānast
hamānā ka'aba-e-hindostānast

The (supreme) place of worship for
the conch-blowers,

surely, (Banaras) is the Kaaba
of Hindustan.

48.

butānash rā hayūlā sholā-e-tūr
sarāpā nūr-e-īzad chashm-e-bad dūr

The idolatrous beauties (of Banaras)
are made of the fire of Tur,[18]

with god-given glow from head to toe.
may they be safe from the evil eye.

---

[18] Fire of Tur: It is a reference to the Qur'anic account of Musa's encounter with Allah near the mountain of Tur, where Allah presents Himself in the form of fire to Musa. This is analogous to God presenting Himself as the burning bush to Moses in the Bible.

49.

meyānhā nāzuk-o-dilhā tawānā
ze nādānī be kār-e-khesh dānā

With delicate waists but strong hearts,
they are wise beyond their years.

50.

tabassum baske dar lab hā tabī'īst
dahan hā rashk-e-gulhā-e-rabī'īst

The smile that forever stays on their lips
is their nature—

thus, their mouths are the envy
of spring blooms.

51.

adā-e-yak-gulistāñ jalwah sarshār
kharame-sad qayāmat fitnah darbār

Their graces are the intoxication
of a garden full of flowers,

their gait is a hundred mischiefs
that spells our doom.

52.

be lutf az mauj-e-gauhar narm rū tar
bināz az khūn-e-'āshiq garm rū tar

Their elegance is gentler
than a wave carrying a pearl,

their youth flows faster than blood
in a lover's vein.

53.

ze-angez-e-qad andāz-e-kharāme
ba-pāe gulbune gustardah dāme

Their stature grants them
an easy, graceful gait,

like webs (of petals) strewn
underneath rose bushes.

54.

ze rangīñ jalwahā ghārtagar-e-hosh
bahār-e-bistar-o-nauroz-e-āghosh

With their colourful ways,
they drive us out of our mind;

they are springtime in bed,
the Nowruz is their embrace.

55.

ze-tāb-e-jalwā-e-khesh ātish afroz
butān-e-but-parast-o-barhaman-soz

With the glow of their appearance,
they fuel the fires (of desire),

these idols who worship statues[19]
singe the Brahmin's heart.

---

[19] 'Idol' is used here in the sense of admired or desired people (probably
the women of Banaras in this case). The Persian-Urdu tradition uses
idols as *but* or lovers as *sanam* for beloveds and statues interchangeably
with intentional ambiguity. Loving a beloved person or idol more than
or before God can be a Sufi means to approach God. It is also taboo and
heretical in orthodox Islam.

56.

bisāmān-e-do 'ālam gulsitāñ rañg
zitāb-e-rukh chirāghān-e-lab-e-gang

With the glow of the two worlds,
their face is coloured like gardens in bloom,

their incandescence lights lamps
on the banks of the Ganga.

57.

rasāñdah az adā-e-shust-u-shūey
bahar mauj-e-navīd-e-ābrūey

Their gestures of bathing
grant

each wave
the good tidings of honour.

58.

qayāmat-qāmatāñ mizhgāñ dar āz āñ
ze mizhgāñ bar saf-e-dil nezah-bāzāñ

Their height, their eyelashes
will cause (our) doom.

these lashes cut,
they spear the frontlines of the heart.

59.

ba tan sarmāyah-e-afzāish-e-dil
sarāpā muzhdah-e-āsāish-e-dil

In body, the capital
of the heart's gladdening,

from head to toe—
relief for the heart.

60.

ba-mastī mauj rā farmūda ārām
ze-naghzī āb rā bakhshīda añdām

Their joy stuns the waves
(of the Ganga) to stillness.

their newness grants
shape to the body of water.

61.

fatādah shorish-e dar qālib-e-āb
ze māhī ṣad dilash dar-sīnah betāb

Embodied by water,
they cause a storm in the river,

a hundred fish hearts
beat in the chest (of the lover).

62.

ze-bas arz-e-tamannā mī kunad gang
ze-mauj āghosh-hā wāmī kunad gang

(As they step into it),
the Ganga reveals its desires;

each wave rises,
opening its arms in embrace.

63.

ze-tāb-e-jalwah-hā betāb gashtah
guhar-hā dar sadaf-hā āb gashtah

Made restless by the lustre
of their radiance,

pearls melt into water
in their shells.

64.

magar goī banāras shāhide hast
ze-gangash subh-o-shām āīnā dar dast

Or one could behold Banaras,
perhaps, as the beauty

who preens from dawn to dusk
with the Ganga as a mirror in their hand.

65.

niyāz-e-aks-e-rūe āñ parī chahr
falak dar zar giraft āīna az mahr

As an offering to catch the reflection
of this angel-faced (city),

the sky has cast the mirror
of the sun in gold.

66.

binām-e-īzad zahe husn-o-jamālash
ke dar āīna mī raqsad misālash

In the name of God,
what beauty and elegance,

even the image (of Banaras)
dances in the looking glass, an exemplar.

67.

bahāristān-e-husn-e-lāobālīst
ba-kishwar-hā samar dar be-misālīst

This (city) is the land
of carefree beauty and spring,

all countries speak of it,
find it nonpareil.

68.

ba-gangash 'aks tā partau fagan shud
banāras khud nazīr kheshtan shud

With its image reflected
in the Ganga,

Banaras is its own
peerless second.

69.

chū dar āīnā-e-ābash namūdañd
gazañd-e-chashm-e-zakhm az we rabūdañd

When it revealed its face
in the mirror of water,

the ritual was completed,
the evil eye avoided.

70.

ba-chīñ nabuwad nigāristāñ chū ūī
ba-gītī nīst shāristān chū ūī

Even in China there is
no such gallery of beauties,

no villa comes close the world over,
no garden, no haven.

71.

bayābāñ-dar-bayābāñ lālah-zārash
gulistāñ dar gulistāñ nau-bahārash

Its forest after forest
is filled with beds of tulips,

its garden after garden
blooms with perpetual spring.

72.

shabe pursīdam az raushan bayāne
ze-gardish hāe gardūñ rāz dāne

One night I asked a (dervish) clairvoyant
who was familiar

with the dance of the skies
(and the secrets of stars).

73.

keh bīnī nekuī-hā az jahāñ raft
wafā-o-mahr-o-āzarm az mayāñ raft

That you see goodness
has left this world,

love, faith and kindness
have left no trace.

74.

ze īmāñhā bajuz nāme namāndah
baghair az dānā-o-dāme namāndah

Faith and creed remain
only in name,

no work is done without
webs of lies and deceit.

75.

pidarhā tishnā-e-khūn-e-pisarhā
pisarhā dushman-e-jān-e-pidarhā

Fathers are thirsty for the blood
of their sons,

sons are bloodthirsty enemies
to their fathers.

76.

barādar-bā-barādar dar-satezast
wifāq az shash-jihat rū dar gurezast

Brother fights brother,
harmony everywhere is in flight.

77.

badīñ be pardgī hāe 'alāmat
chirā paidā namī gardad qayāmat

When so many such signs
abound unveiled,

why is Doomsday
not here already?

78.

binafkh-e-sūr taʾwīq az pae chīst
qayāmat rā-ʾināñ gīr-e-junūñ kīst

Why is there a delay in (Isrāfil)[20]
blowing the trumpet of doom?[21]

Who has stopped Judgement Day
in its tracks?

---

[20] The fourth major angel in Islam (Cf. Raphael in Christianity) who will
  blow the trumpet of doomsday. He may be construed as an angel of
  music too.
[21] Isrāfil would blow the *sūr*, which may be thought of as a trumpet,
  signalling the doom on Judgement Day.

79.

sūe kāshī bā indāz-e-ishārat
tabassum kard-o-guftā īñ 'imārat

Pointing to Kashi
with a gesture, he smiled

and said: it is for the sake
of this town.

80.

keh haqqā nīst ṣāneʾ rā gawārā
keh az ham rezad īñ rañgīñ bínārā

It is unbearable
to the Maker—

that this colourful city
be razed.

81.

bulañd uftādah tamkīn-e-banāras
buwad bar auj-e-ū andeshah nā ras

So great is the majesty
of Banaras,

that the reach of thought
cannot mount its summit.

82.

ilā ai ghālib-e-kār uftādah
zechashm-e-yār-o-aghyār uftādah

O, Ghalib, you
good for nothing, you,

in the eyes of friends and strangers,
you have fallen low.

83.

zekhesh-o-āshnā begānah gashteh
junūñ gul karda-o-dīwānah gashteh

You've become a stranger
to friends and family,

you've gone raving mad,
what's this lunacy!

84.

che-mah-shar sarzad az āb-o-gil-e-to
dareghā az tū-o-āh az di-le-to

What tumult rises from your make-up
of dirt and water?

Alas, woe is you, and pity
for your heart too.

85.

che-jūe jalwā zīñ rañgīñ chaman hā
bahisht-e-khesh shau az khūñ shudan hā

What need have you
of the splendours of this garden (of Kashi)?

Become your heaven out of your grief,
your heart's blood.

86.

junūnat gar ba-nafs-e-khud tamāmast
ze-kāshī tābeh kāshāñ nīm gāmast

When your madness reaches
the perfect frenzy,[22]

Kashan[23] from Kashi
is just a half-step journey.

---

[22] There is a hint of Sufi divine madness that attains perfection and so union with God here.

[23] Kashan: a famous city of Iran, the residents of which were also called Kashi. Ghalib is connecting two major cities of Persia and India here in this verse through a Persianate cosmopolitanism and thus emphasizing a continuity of civilizations.

87.

chū bū-e-gul ze pairāhan barūñ āī
ze āzādī zi-band-e-tan barūñ āī

Like fragrance from a rose, exude
from your shirt,

break the bonds of your body
and be free.

88.

madeh az kaf tarīq-e-ma'rifat rā
sarat gardam bigard īñ shash jehat rā

Don't let go of the path
to true knowledge—

look around,
scour the six directions.

89.

firaumāndan bakāshī nāresāīst
khudārā iñ che kāfir mājrāīst

To dither and delay in Kashi
is frailty,[24]

by God, it is
profanity.

---

[24] As Ghalib ran the risk of losing sight of his main goal of reaching Calcutta.

90.

azīñ da'wā ba-ātish shūī lab rā
bi-khāñ ghamnāma-e-zauq-e-talab rā

For the claim you make,
rinse your mouth with fire,

and read the letter of sorrows (from home)
seeking your presence, full of ardour, desire.

91.

bikāshī lakht-e-az kāshānah yād ār
darīñ jannat azāñ wīrānah yād ār

Think of what happened at home,
while you were in Kashi,[25]

what became of that ruin
while you were in this heaven.

---

[25] Ghalib puns and alliterates on Kāshi and kāshānah (home) in the original
hemistich, which must unfortunately be lost in translation.

92.

daregha dar watan wāmāndah-e-chañd
bi-khūn-e-dīdah zauraq rāñdah-e-chañd

Your forlorn folk await you
in your country, alas!

they row their boats in blood
that springs from their eyes.

93.

hawas rā pāe dar dāman shikastah
ba-ummīd-e-tū chashm az khesh bastah

.

They have folded their hopeful legs
into their chests,

given up their hopes
built upon you and closed their eyes.

94.

ba-shahr az bekasī sahrā nashīnāñ
ba-rūe-ātish-e-dil jāguzīnāñ

In their misery, even the city where they live
feels like a wilderness.

They lead their lives comforted
by the flame burning in their hearts.

95.

magar kāñ qaum rā dahr āfrīdah
ze-sīmāb-e-bar-ātish ārmīdah

The universe appears to have
sculpted these people

with mercury that quivers
forever in the flame.

96.

hamāh dār khāk-o-khūñ afgandah-e-to
bahukm-e-bekasī hā bañdah-e-to

They lie in blood and dirt,
at your hands,

ruled by helplessness,
they're slaves in your hold.

97.

chū shama' az dāghh-e-dil āzar fashānāñ
ba-bazm-e-'arz-e-da'wā be-zabānāñ

They light the flame
from the scars on their hearts,

but do not let a complaint
reach the tip of their tongues.

98.

sar-o-sarmāyah ghārat kardah-e-to
ze-to nālāñ wale dar pardah-e-to

You're the cause behind
the loss of all their belongings;

they lament their faith in you
but don't let it show.

99.

az ānānat taghāful khushnumā nīst
ba-dāgh-e-shāñ hawā-e-gul rawā nīst

It is not good
that you forget them,

while their hearts are scarred,
you chase blossoms.

100.

turā ai bekhabar kārīst darpesh
bayābāne wa kohsārīst darpesh

Oh you carefree (man),
work lies ahead,

forests and mountains—
both lie ahead.

101.

chu-sailābat shatābāñ mī tawāñ raft
bayābāñ-dar-bayābāñ mī tawāñ raft

You must go surging forth
like a deluge;

you must cross
wilderness, deserts, forests alike.

102.

turā ze-andoh majnūñ būd bāyad
kharāb-e-koh-o-hāmūñ būd bāyad

By now you should have become
a Majnūñ drowned in grief,[26]

ruined yourself roaming
mountains and plains.

---

[26] Majnūñ: Means the mad or crazy one in Arabic. It is what the seventh-century poet-lover Qais ibn al-Mullawah was called by the people after he went mad for his beloved Laila bint-Mahdi (also known as Laila al-Amiriya). The story from Arabic lore has passed through from Persian into Indian languages and also exists in Turkish and other languages. Lord Byron, the British Romantic, called them 'Mejnoun and Leila, the Romeo and Juliet of the East' in his poem, *The Giaour*. They were originally made famous by the *Khamsa* or the *Panj Ganj* (written as five long poems c. 1163–1197 AD) of Nizami Ganjavi, the Persian poet.

103.

tan āsānī ba-tārāj-e-balādah
chū bīnī rañj-e-khud rā rūnumādah

Discard the comforts of your body
to the pillage of misfortunes;

if obstacles remain, offer yourself as tribute
to ward off the evil eye.

104.

hawas rā sar babālīn-e-fanā nah
nafas rā az dil ātish zer-e-pā nah

Give all your desire and greed
to death,

and with the fire of your heart,
kindle your breath.

105.

dil az tāb-e-balā bagodāz-o-khūñ kun
zidānish kār nagushāyad junūñ kun

In the heat of adversity,
melt your heart into blood;

if reason be of no help,
get into a frenzy, go mad.

106.

nafas tākhud faro na-nashīnad az pāe
dame az jādah-paimāe mayā sāe

Till your last breath,
stay on your feet,

do not for a moment
stop walking the road.

107.

sharār āsā fanā āmādah bar khez
bayafshāñ dāman-o-āzādah bar khez

Rise to be extinguished
in an instant like a spark,

dust your shirt
be free.

108.

ze illā dam zan-o-taslīm-e-lā sho
bugo allāh-o-barq-e-māsiwā sho

Breathe of *illā*—'exception',
and accept *lā*—'denial',

say 'Allah', and like lightning
extinguish the rest.